ONE WEEK LOAN

WOMEN'S HUMAN RIGHTS AND CULTURE

From Deadlock to Dialogue

Rikki Holtmaat
Jonneke Naber

intersentia
Cambridge – Antwerp – Portland

Distribution for the UK:
Hart Publishing Ltd.
16C Worcester Place
Oxford OX1 2JW
UK
Tel.: +44 1865 51 75 30
Email: mail@hartpub.co.uk

Distribution for the USA and Canada:
International Specialized Book Services
920 NE 58th Ave. Suite 300
Portland, OR 97213
USA
Tel.: +1 800 944 6190 (toll free)
Tel.: +1 503 287 3093
Email: info@isbs.com

Distribution for Austria:
Neuer Wissenschaftlicher Verlag
Argentinierstraße 42/6
1040 Wien
Austria
Tel.: +43 1 535 61 03 24
Email: office@nwv.at

Distribution for other countries:
Intersentia Publishers
Groenstraat 31
2640 Mortsel
Belgium
Tel.: +32 3 680 15 50
Email: mail@intersentia.be

Women's Human Rights and Culture
Rikki Holtmaat and Jonneke Naber

Cover illustration: Anna van Schelven, www.panannа.nl

ISBN 978-94-000-0137-4
D/2010/7849/135
NUR 828

FOREWORD / ACKNOWLEDGEMENTS

This book builds on a research paper that was written in 2009 for persons and organisations that are directly or indirectly working for the Dutch Ministers of Foreign Affairs and Development Co-operation. The assignment to write this paper was part of a wider project, subsidised by the Dutch Ministry of Foreign Affairs (DMH-MR), on the theme "*Women's Human Rights & Culture/Tradition/ Religion*". (See also Holtmaat & Boerefijn 2010.)

Prof. dr. Rikki Holtmaat holds a chair in International Non-Discrimination Law at Leiden University. Jonneke Naber, LLM, was temporarily associated with Leiden University for the purpose of the project and has a lot of experience in the area of development co-operation and human rights. The authors undertook their research independently of the Ministry of Foreign Affairs. The content of this book therefore does not necessarily reflect the position of the Ministry in the debate about women's human rights and culture.

The book is based on a study of the relevant international documents concerning women's human rights, and of the interpretation thereof by the most important supervising bodies and implementing agencies. In addition, we have reviewed the (often heated) discussions in the area of women's human rights and culture that currently take place in international academia. This discussion is very extensive; therefore we do not pretend to have covered all publications in this area, nor to give a full account of all possible perspectives on the issue. Our main sources can be traced in our footnotes and in the bibliography. Apart from this desk study, we have conducted interviews, in person, by telephone and via e-mail, with a number of resource persons working in the area of implementing women's human rights in various countries all over the world, including The Netherlands. Although not often quoted literally, their observations and recommendations have found their way into the book.

The authors are deeply grateful to the Dutch Ministry of Foreign Affairs who made this book possible. Although we were in the position to do our work independently, we have greatly appreciated discussions at the Ministry in meetings with various experts in the field of implementation of women's human rights. We also thank all other persons who have delivered valuable input through the interviews. And we sincerely hope that, in return, they may take profit of our work.

CONTENTS

ABBREVIATIONS

CEDAW	Convention on the Elimination of all forms of Discrimination Against Women
CERD	Convention on the Elimination of Racial Discrimination
CO	Concluding Observations (CEDAW)
CRC	Convention on the Rights of the Child
DEDAW	Declaration on the Elimination of Discrimination against Women
DEVAW	Declaration on the Elimination of Violence Against Women
ECHR	European Convention on Human Rights
GR	General Recommendation (CEDAW)
ICCPR	International Covenant on Civil and Political Rights
ICRPD	International Convention on the Rights of Persons with Disabilities
ICSECR	International Covenant on Economic, Social and Cultural Rights
UDHR	Universal Declaration of Human Rights
UN	United Nations
UNFPA	United Nations Population Fund
UNHRC	United Nations Human Rights Committee / Council
VAW	Violence Against Women

CHAPTER 1
INTRODUCTION

"The challenge is to ensure that the right to pursue, develop and preserve culture in all its manifestations is in consonance with and serves to uphold the universality, indivisibility and interdependence of all human rights. This includes the right not to be forced into participation."[1]

1.1 CULTURE BLOCKING THE IMPLEMENTATION OF WOMEN'S HUMAN RIGHTS

In many of today's discussions about the difficulties that surround the implementation of women's human rights[2], issues related to culture, religion, custom or tradition pop up. 'Culture'[3] is being blamed for bad behaviour.[4] Bad behaviour, not only of those who use culture as an excuse to commit serious violations of women's human rights, but also of governments who refuse to implement women's human rights standards, arguing that their culture forces them to accept limited interpretations of international human rights obligations, or to reject such obligations altogether.[5] It is often male representatives or leaders of certain religious, ethnic or cultural groups that determine and declare that their culture does not allow them to acknowledge women's equality; women's own opinions on this topic are in most instances not voiced or not heard. Yakin Ertürk, the UN Special Rapporteur on violence against women, observes that: "(...) despite the fact that the international community has recognized the

---

1 Farida Shaheed, Independent United Nations Expert in the field of Cultural Rights in her first press statement, dd 23 November 2009. See: www.ohchr.org/en/NewsEvents/Pages/DisplayNews.aspx?NewsID=9619&LangID=e (last accessed on July 20, 2010).

2 Throughout this book, we use the term 'women's human rights' or 'the human rights of women', instead of 'women's rights', in order to underline that we refer to upholding *human* rights values and norms for women as equals to men, and not to some specific set of rights for women-only.

3 For the sake of brevity in the remainder of this book we write 'culture' (without the citation marks) as the overall term encompassing religion/customs/tradition *and* culture in a more restricted sense. See also Chapter 3, para. 3.1.

4 Volpp 2000.

5 See e.g. the discussions on the national and international level about the Afghanistan Draft Law against Shia women, www.guardian.co.uk/world/2009/aug/14/afghanistan-womens-rights-rape (last accessed on December 10, 2009).

universality of rights, identity politics and cultural relativist paradigms are increasingly employed to constrain in particular the rights of women."[6] This experience is shared by the Dutch government:

> "[W]ithin the various international human rights forums, the universality of human rights is being called into question by a growing number of states, and specific cultural or religious circumstances are being forcefully invoked in order to curtail universality. (...) This trend is also noticeable in the political dialogues on human rights which the Netherlands conducts at multilateral and bilateral level (...)."[7]

Any such 'cultural defence' poses severe difficulties for international organisations and national governments, who, in their work on development co-operation, humanitarian aid or peace keeping operations, advocate for the implementation of women's human rights. Many local officials and international and national non-governmental organisations (NGOs) run into the same difficulties. An appeal to culture usually is "not questioned and takes on an aura of morality."[8] Besides, such an appeal is often accompanied with a reference to neo-colonialism or imperialism, which is a reproach that most (Western) people don't like to hear.

The reaction of the 'outside world' (i.e. outside the particular culture itself), may be twofold.[9] It may stop interfering with the particular culture which resists implementing women's human rights and stop pressing for cultural change in the name of valuing or sustaining a wide diversity of cultures, declaring that no ranking of cultures is possible (cultural relativist perspective). Or it may hammer on the legal obligation to implement internationally agreed universal legal standards concerning women's equality and non-discrimination of women (universality perspective). The first reaction means the end of the discussion, because the argument that a particular culture prevents the full implementation of women's human rights is accepted without any further inquiry.

---

6 UN Special Rapporteur on Violence Against Women (VAW), Report on 'Intersections between culture and violence against women', 17 January 2007, UN Doc. A/HRC/4/34, para. 68. See also the Address of the Dutch Human Rights Ambassador, Arjan Hamburger, at the Colloquium on *Women's Human Rights and Culture/Religion/Tradition*, held in The Hague, 12 May 2009 (Hamburger 2010).

7 Letter of the Dutch Minister of Foreign Affairs and Minister for Development Co-operation to Advisory Council on International Affairs, 'Request for advice on Reclaiming the Universality of Human Rights', 21 May 2008. See also Government Response of 24 March 2009 to Advice of Advisory Council on International Affairs 'Universality of Human Rights. Principles, Practice and Prospects' (November 2008), p 3, Dutch only.

8 Office of the High Commissioner for Human Rights 'Fact Sheet No.23, Harmful Traditional Practices Affecting the Health of Women and Children'; See: www.ohchr.org/Documents/Publications/FactSheet23en.pdf (last accessed on July 20, 2010).

9 These are the two extremes. Of course mixed reactions are also possible. It is the aim of this book to investigate such middle positions.

The second reaction does also not guarantee a successful strategy of cultural change. This is because it is not enough to simply confront the other party with the international legal obligation to implement women's human rights. According to international law, these rights have to be respected under all circumstances by all nations in the world.[10] This approach to human rights, however principled and firm it may seem, often leads to 'outsiders' claiming to know exactly what is right or good for 'women-of-culture'. In that way, human rights advocates often present women's human rights as a fixed and static set of international legal norms, about which no further discussion is possible.[11] At the same time they "see themselves and their projects as rooted in modernity and envision culture as the obstacle."[12] In that way, universality becomes an inflexible form of uniformity, thereby blocking a dynamic and progressive implementation of women's human rights.[13] Again, in many instances women's own concerns and perspectives are not included in such firm and principled human rights approaches.

In the end, both culture and human rights are frequently being presented as something monolithic and static, and as something that contains an unchangeable and everlasting essence or truth or absolute norms or values. This inevitably leads to a deadlock in the discussion: both sides firmly locked up in their position of the immutability of culture and/or of women's human rights. In this way, a clash or incompatibility between women's human rights and culture is constructed, which leads to a discussion between the deaf, or to no discussion at all.

We think that a more effective approach needs to be developed, one in which the central focus is how to enhance a fruitful dialogue about women's human rights and culture. In the literature about this issue a cross-cultural or intercultural dialogue is often proposed.[14] However, this suggestion mostly remains quite abstract and general, without specifying *how* this method could be applied. Therefore, in this book, the we address the following question:

> **How can a firm deadlock between on the one hand women's human rights and on the other hand culture be avoided? *Or, to put it positively*: How can we enhance a fruitful dialogue about women's human rights and culture?**

---

10 In the international arena the human rights of women are being considered as universal, indivisible and interdependent. See the motto for this Chapter. See also the Vienna Declaration of Human Rights, 12 July 1993, UN Doc. A/CONF.157/23.

11 This reproach is often made of e.g. Susan Moller Okin's seminal article: 'Why multiculturalism is bad for women'. See Moller Okin 1997.

12 Merry 2003 Polar. She adds that this tendency "is enhanced by their commitment to a model of legal rationality, an idea that is incompatible with celebrating local cultural diversity."

13 See further para. 4.1, where we discuss debates about universality and cultural relativity.

14 E.g. Shachar 2001, Merry 2008, Philips 2007, Nyamu 2000 and An Na'im 1990.

In putting this question at the centre, we do not suggest that at this moment in time everywhere in the diplomatic service, or in the activities and projects of organisations who are working in the area of development co-operation, humanitarian aid or peace keeping actions, discussions on this issue are completely blocked. There are many examples of successful projects in which international and national partners work fruitfully together with the aim of improving women's conditions of life, and have little difficulty in understanding each other. It is from such projects that we draw examples in this book, in order to demonstrate how a clash or a deadlock may be avoided or overcome.

We are aware that having a dialogue will not solve all problems that surround the implementation of international women's human rights standards. We fully acknowledge that in some cases other means, such as diplomatic pressure, international accountability procedures (like e.g. investigations by Special Rapporteurs, or individual complaints procedures before the Human Rights Committee or the CEDAW Committee), national litigation or other forms of pressure on national governments, are (also) indicated. In the end, however, we believe that engaging into a real dialogue about women's human rights and culture is the most effective strategy to stimulate the necessary cultural change that will allow women all over the world to lead a life in which their human rights – including their right to participate in their culture – are respected.

1.2 THE HUMAN RIGHTS APPROACH TO CULTURE

We have approached our research from the perspective of international human rights law. This means that we presume that internationally agreed standards about the inherent equality and dignity of women can inform us about the nature of the relationship between on the one hand women's human rights and on the other hand the right (also of women!) to freedom of religion and respect for culture and tradition. These two sets of rights are often presented as clashing or opposite fundamental rights that in principle have an equal standing or equal weight.[15] In such a 'clashing rights' discourse, it is very difficult to come to a decision about which of them prevails. In order to arrive at a solution, the question then becomes whether one of the two rights possibly (under certain conditions) might outweigh the other. In other words, the central (legal) question becomes whether it is possible, by invoking cultural, traditional or religious

15 Baer (2010, p 64) rightfully points out that any such 'clashing rights' discourse is based on the belief that legal rights do have a fixed and determined meaning, and are not sites for struggle over meaning: "Any given law and any given set of rights, including human rights, are contested and, if taken seriously as sites of diverse interpretations, are not useful to mark clear collisions, i.e. of religious freedom and equality."

rights, to set aside the human rights of women. Or, the other way around, whether the internationally agreed human rights of women may form a firewall or barrier against offences or violations of women's most fundamental rights that are based on or are justified with an appeal to culture. Since the aim of this book is to find roads to a fruitful dialogue about women's human rights and culture, we have avoided this particular language of clashing rights. Instead, from the very beginning we want to stress that part of women's human rights is their right to fully and equally participate in the interpretation and development of the culture to which they choose to belong. Therefore, any dialogue about women's human rights and culture should be an *inclusive* dialogue, i.e. including women's own perspectives and concerns in this regard.

The book not only describes the existing international legal norms concerning women's human rights, some research has also gone into the question of what have proven to be best practices, in terms of engaging into a real and fruitful dialogue about culture and women's human rights. How, in other words, can international human rights law be incorporated into these discussions in such a way that a deadlock is avoided? And what other (than strictly legal) arguments may also be used or may even be more effective for engaging into a constructive dialogue about this issue? The goal, in the end, is to keep the conversation about women's human rights and culture going, instead of 'telling each other the truth'.

1.3 WOMEN'S HUMAN RIGHTS AND THE DEVELOPMENT OF WOMEN

In past decades, people have become more and more aware of the fact that the full realisation of women's human rights is related to the level of economical, social, political, administrative and legal development of any country.[16] Gender inequality is strongly correlated with poverty.[17] Therefore, an important way of improving the status of women is to stimulate the general development of a country. However, not in one society (wealthy or poor) are women's human rights fully protected, nor do women enjoy the same opportunities as men. It has shown that national income is not a decisive factor for improvement in this area. In many cases, a strong political commitment has driven efforts to enhance

16 The academic and policy discussion about the relationship between 'development' and 'human rights' (or sometimes called: 'the human rights based approach to development') is extensive. See for an influential contribution to this 'project' the Volume edited by Alston & Robinson 2004; see also Alston 2005; Sano 2000, and Uvin 2000.

17 See "Human Development Indicators, Table 28 Gender related Development Index", *Human Development Report 2007–2008*, United Nations Development Programme, New York 2007, p 326.

women's human development despite a shortage of resources. In addition, it must be remarked that the reverse is also true: the implementation of women's human rights is a crucial precondition for a country's development.[18] For these reasons, this book mainly focuses on *the human rights based approach* to the elimination of all forms of discrimination against women, though acknowledging that "[U]nless women's agency is recognised and their capabilities supported through social, economic and political empowerment the human rights they are promised will remain abstract concepts."[19] In our view, strategies to improve women's conditions of life can only be effective if they focus on a strengthening of women's human economic, social and political position (development) as well as of their human rights, in order to enable them to fully use all of their human capabilities.[20] Both processes need to incorporate women's concerns and take away the obstacles for the enjoyment of their human rights, thereby improving women's opportunities to lead a full and meaningful life as a human being.

Presenting the issue as an 'either-or-choice' between women's human rights and the development of women leads to a false image of both of them. Any human rights based approach includes civil and political rights as well as economic, social and cultural rights of women. Especially the latter type of human rights can only be realised with the help of extensive and effective development co-operation policies. In addition to this, the concept of the human right to development clearly has important gender dimensions. We take the stance that using the language of international law forms a crucial input in the difficult debate about women's human rights and development in the light of culture. This makes this book relevant for all those national and international, governmental and non-governmental organisations or agencies that want to develop policies of supporting and sustaining women's human rights and policies in the area of contributing to the improvement of women's actual conditions of life.

1.4 THE AUDIENCE WE INTEND TO REACH

With this book we seek to offer a contribution to the difficult and slow process of implementing women's human rights. Often government officials run into the problem of having to propagate and defend their Ministry of Foreign Affairs' human rights policies against discussion partners who, in different forms and with a variety of arguments, openly or implicitly resist against such policies on

18 See e.g. the Dutch Ministry of Foreign Affairs' Policy paper 'Human dignity for all. A human rights strategy for foreign policy', p 43. Submitted to Parliament on 5 November 2007 (TK 31 263, nr.1).

19 Report of the UN Special Rapporteur on VAW, 'Political economy of women's human rights', UN Doc. A/HRC/11/6, 18 May 2009, para. 2.

20 Nussbaum 2000.

the basis of their culture. Sometimes these partners use the argument that women's human rights are Western[21], or even imperialist or neo-colonialist.[22] Persons or organisations working in the field of humanitarian aid, development co-operation, human rights affairs or in the area of armed conflict intervention may experience similar difficulties. In order to enhance the progressive implementation of women's human rights, it is important for all of these actors to learn about how to respond to cultural, religious, customary or traditional objections against women's equality. This book is meant to help them with the difficult task of finding solid and dissuasive arguments in favour of women's human rights and presenting these arguments in such a way that they will keep the dialogue with their discussion partners going.

We realise that our readers have many different backgrounds. In the book we explain crucial concepts, such as women's human rights and culture or gender, at a basic level, however at the same time enhancing a deep and thorough understanding of these concepts in order to improve the quality of the dialogue about the issue.[23] Therefore, both the Chapter on the Human Rights of Women and the Chapter on Culture and Gender provide the background information which is needed for a good understanding of what is at stake when engaging into such a dialogue. What do we actually mean when we say 'human rights' and what are the profound and persistent resistances against women's equality? How does culture relate to gender? And why is an essentialist approach to both culture/gender and human rights so utterly ineffective? We expect that this book is informative for individual actors who advocate for women's human rights – including the human right of women to participate in determining and changing their culture – and that it will also facilitate and stimulate the exchange of helpful insights and good practices on the issue at hand.

---

21 See e.g. Pollis & Schwab 1979, arguing that human rights are Western constructs and have limited applicability in the rest of the world.

22 See on this stance Otto 1997.

23 The book provides the reader with the manifold sources of our findings in the literature and– most importantly – in international documents. We have chosen to reveal these sources, because having them at hand may be helpful for those who want to continue to study these issues. However, at the same time the book is meant to be very practical, in the sense that it concentrates on the question *how* a dialogue could be enhanced or facilitated. Human rights theory, gender theory and legal argumentation are explained in quite some detail in order to support a more effective actual implementation of women's human rights norms.

CHAPTER 2
WOMEN'S HUMAN RIGHTS

"Gender inequality is the single biggest challenge to the international human rights system."[1]

"Regardless of a universal sex-equality norm, women's reality is one of gross inequality."[2]

In order to answer the question how one can enhance a fruitful dialogue about women's human rights and culture, it is important to first gain a good understanding of what is meant by women's human rights and why a clash between or incompatibility of these rights and (a right to) culture is conceivable at all. For that purpose, we place women's human rights in the wider general human rights framework. In the first part of this Chapter, the normative nature and legal stature of human rights is discussed; this includes a brief account of the historical and philosophical background of the very concept of human rights itself, and what the acceptance of such rights means for the relations between sovereign States parties.[3] This may help to recognise the particular legal and normative character of human rights, developed as a way out of historically experienced oppressions caused by policies and practices of discrimination.[4] Human rights are about achieving greater inclusiveness for *all* human beings. Seeking increasing acceptance of the human rights of women fits logically into this process. Moreover, in this Chapter it is explained that throughout history there has been quite a lapse of time between particular human rights' first pronouncements and their practical realisation. The difficult implementation of women's human rights is exemplary to this.

---

1 Philip Alston, voiced at a special panel of the Human Rights Council, June 8, 2009. See: www.ohchr.org/EN/NEWSEVENTS/Pages/InequalityBeforeLaw.aspx (last accessed on July 20, 2010).

2 Hernández-Truyol 2002, p 145.

3 For a complete overview of existing international treaties and of mechanisms of international supervision we refer our readers to commentaries and case books on international human rights law. Instead, we concentrate on those features of human rights doctrine and practice that are important for our question how a fruitful dialogue about women's human rights and culture may be enhanced.

4 Winston 2007.

The second part of the Chapter contains an introduction to the Convention on the Elimination of All forms of Discrimination Against Women (CEDAW), as the main international legal document in which women's human rights have been codified. CEDAW contains important norms as regards culture and women's human rights, which are discussed in the third part of this Chapter. In the final part we turn to other international legal documents that might clarify the difficult relationship between women's human rights and culture. In that context it is discussed whether there exists such a thing as a right to culture, and how this right is developed and circumscribed in international law.

2.1 THE NORMATIVE NATURE AND LEGAL STATURE OF HUMAN RIGHTS

FROM THE EXERCISE OF ABSOLUTE POWER TO DEMOCRATIC CITIZENSHIP RIGHTS

In order for human rights norms to be conceivable on the international level, first the concept of citizenship rights had to be developed at the national level. Less than three hundred years ago hardly anywhere on our planet could a human being safely rely on the State where he/she lived to protect his/her property and life against arbitrary and random claims or punishments by State authorities. Nor did every (adult) inhabitant or subject have any real influence on how the State was to be organised and what its economical, political and military goals and priorities should be. Before the French and American Revolutions, at the end of the 18th Century, there was little protection against abuse of power by the State, be it brutal physical power (to the extreme of applying capital punishment without due legal process), or legal power, which was authorised by autocratic laws from absolutist monarchs or from an economic, religious or nobility elite that exclusively ruled the country. During and after these Revolutions, the exercise of governmental power became normatively restrained by the acceptance of a set of basic citizenship rights, including basic or fundamental civil and political rights.[5] It meant a new ordering of society on the basis of a 'social contract' between autonomous and free citizens and the State, in which the first gave up their most fundamental (natural) right to be free from any State interference and the latter in turn guaranteed the safety, peace and prosperity of all. Creating and guaranteeing citizenship rights became the core of the constitutional and political organisation of society. Most importantly, they entailed the right to political participation and the right to vote, and the right not to be deprived of property or life without due process. Other fundamental

5 In this sense, the idea of human rights has a Western origin, meaning that *de facto* they were first *officially* declared in Western territories. See Bielefeldt 2000, p 100.

rights are the right to (political) association, and to freedom of speech and of religion/conscious. The proclamation of citizenship rights thus lead to significant, revolutionary shifts of power from absolutist to democratic governments with the rule of law and a division of countervailing powers.

FROM HIERARCHY TO EQUALITY

One of the basic idea(l)s of the 18th Century revolutions was the principle of equality of all human beings.[6] The acceptance of the idea(l) of *equality of all citizens*[7] meant a clear break with past social relationships which were structured according to a *hierarchy* from kingdom to slavery. Until the end of the Middle Ages – at least in the Western world – it was completely normal *not* to consider fellow human beings as being equal in dignity and rights.[8] A person's social, economic and legal status was determined by his or her birth into a certain class or caste, religion, ethnicity or race, or nation. A person's biological sex to a major degree determined whether he or she was capable of being a bearer of rights at all. Slavery did not need a special justification, nor did sexual and other forms of exploitation of women, children and (mentally) disabled persons. On the contrary: such *unequal* human relations were deemed natural, pre-destined or God-given. In the course of time, within the context of the construction of the democratic nation State and the rule of law, equality became a most fundamental principle; it was seen as constitutive for legality as such. Equality in and before the law, without preferential treatment / discrimination on the basis of class, ethnicity, race, religion, sex, et cetera, was deemed to be a most fundamental characteristic of the new legal order that gradually came into being in many countries after the 18th Century revolutions.

After first having been accepted (at least in principle – that is: only with respect to white adult male citizens who owned a certain amount of property and were therefore considered as 'deserving' and 'independent') on the national level, the concepts of 'human equality' and of 'fundamental rights of citizens of the State', gradually started to transgress the borders of nation States. It became accepted (by many) that these rights were deemed to *inherently belong to all human beings*, irrespective of where they were born and where they actually lived. Especially the severe atrocities committed against human beings and the experiences of

---

6 Other constitutive principles were / are liberty and brotherhood (solidarity).

7 In fact, this included only human beings who were deemed to be 'rational'; i.e. slaves, colonised peoples, women, children and (mentally) disabled people were excluded from this notion of equality.

8 "In medieval cosmology inequality – including inequality among human beings in their social and legal status – constitutes the very beauty of the hierarchical order of things." Bielefeldt 2000, p 95.

fierce injustice during the period of World War II were an important reason why in the second half of the 20th Century human rights became adopted in official *international law* documents.[9]

THE IDEA OF THE INHERENT VALUE AND DIGNITY OF EACH AND EVERY HUMAN BEING

There is considerable debate in today's world about the origin and/or about the historical development of human rights. Some commentators point to the fact that Christianity laid the basis for the concept of equality, with its belief that 'all humans are equal in the eyes of God'. Others point to (Greek) Stoic philosophy, and/or to the European idea of natural law or the English common law tradition. Still others maintain that similar value orientations can also be found in various parts of the world / world history.[10] The Indian philosopher Sudipta Kaviraj strongly warns against seeing human rights as an automatic result of European history:

> "Indeed, one danger of reading this too deep in the European past is that this encourages essentialist thinking. Achievement of a civil society then gets associated with a mysterious and indefinable feature of European culture or 'Western spirit', which proves before the debate has begun that it is beyond the cultural means of other societies to create similar institutions."[11]

Another pitfall is to describe the history of human rights as a development from pre-modern or traditional societies – not familiar with the concepts of human equality and human rights – to modern or 'posttraditional' societies that (supposedly) have fully embraced these concepts. The German legal philosopher and former Director of the German Human Rights Institute, Heiner Bielefeldt, calls this a problematic assumption because

> "[I]f human rights were to imply an abstract dichotomy between tradition and modernity, then those who continue to cherish their religious or cultural traditions would be conceptually excluded from having full access to human rights. In other words, the acceptance of human rights, at least in principle, would be confined to a circle of people who implicitly or explicitly have broken away from their religious, philosophical, or cultural traditions."[12]

---

9 Winston 2007 and Bielefeldt 2000, p 101.

10 See e.g. Lauren 1999, p 11.

11 Kavaraj 1993, p 81, as cited in Bielefeldt 2000, p 94.

12 Bielefeldt 2000, p 97. In the end, all theories which exclusively base the existence of human rights on a particular tradition boil down to an essentialist view of the particular 'original' culture. It also leads to human rights activists engaging into a 'civilisation mission', directed against 'pre-modern' societies. See also para. 3.3.

No matter the precise origin, a distinguished set of *humanistic*[13] values underlie the 1948 United Nation's *Universal Declaration of Human Rights*, which recognises in its Preamble that "the inherent dignity and of the equal and inalienable rights of all members of the human family is the foundation of freedom, justice and peace in the world". In addition, Article 1 states that "[A]ll human beings are born free and equal in dignity and rights. They are endowed with reason and conscience and should act towards one another in a spirit of brotherhood." The same principles were subsequently adopted in many other international human rights documents.[14] All of them firmly declare that – regardless of their actual differences[15] – *all human beings are equal in rights and in dignity.* In that way, besides equality, human dignity forms a core concept in human rights 'theory'.

The concept of human dignity has got a particular meaning through Western enlightenment philosophy, for which Immanuel Kant laid an important foundation.[16] The inherent value and freedom of each and every human being is put at the very centre of this moral and ethical system of beliefs and practices. In this moral philosophy, human beings are considered to be *ends in themselves.* They may never be used as a *means* or instrument for achieving other people's purposes in life, nor may they be used by the State to achieve its own policies or aims. This puts severe restraints on the way in which a nation State may treat its citizens or inhabitants. *All* human beings in principle are deemed capable of making rational choices of what it means to be living a dignified and worthy life as a human being, without State interference. We call this moral and ethical value orientation *humanistic*, because its basis does not lie in any God-given ordinance or metaphysical order, but in the appreciation of human beings as ontologically rational and autonomous beings.[17] This enlightenment philosophy, in turn, is closely connected to liberalism, in which rationality and individual autonomy are equally put in the centre of the philosophical and political value system.[18]

---

13 See below in this paragraph for the meaning that is attached to this word.

14 See e.g. the Preambles of the ICCPR, ICESCR, CERD, CEDAW and the CRC.

15 Despite the recognition of the fundamental principle of equality of all human beings, it should also be recognised that in fact all human beings are differently situated, i.e. are in different social, geographical, economic, et cetera positions. Recognising these *de facto* differences and enhancing that nevertheless human beings will get equal opportunities to make something of their lives, lies at the basis of the *substantive* principle of equality (as opposed to *formal* equality, in which the inherent (abstract) equality of human beings is the starting point). See also para. 2.2.

16 See Bielefeldt 1997.

17 This is a secular approach to / belief about human nature. Some religions also believe that *all* human beings are rational and autonomous beings, but that these capacities do not lie in human nature as such, but are God-given. Respecting human freedom and autonomy, in such systems of belief, becomes part of respecting Gods creation of the human kind.

18 This political / philosophical liberalism, although related, may not be equated with economic liberalism in its capitalist form.

Underlying the concept of human rights is the presumption that *all* human beings – irrespective of time and place of birth, national or ethnic origin, race, class or caste, sex, sexual orientation, disablement, or any other classification that human beings can possibly construct between themselves – are *dignified* beings, *because* they are potentially rational and responsible persons that have a genuine desire to be in control over their own lives. Not subjugation but participation, not dependency but autonomy, not slavery but freedom, are key notions in this philosophy. This means that it is neither destiny nor fate, but *making your own life plan come true* that is the basic idea behind human rights. Of course, if you wish, you can pursue your life together with others. Human rights is not a plea for egocentrism or solitariness.

The adoption of the Universal Declaration and of subsequent Human Rights treaties did meet with resistance, just as well in the Western world. Many conservative philosophers who deeply criticised enlightenment theory and (political and philosophical) liberalism,[19] but also Catholic and Protestant Christian churches, were strongly opposed to the idea that human beings were put on such high moral pedestal. They made every effort to counter the acceptance of international human rights norms. Heiner Bielefeldt explains that the fact that Christian churches originally were strongly opposed to the idea of human rights and to the human rights legal project "(…) indicates that human rights cannot appropriately be described as an 'organic' result of the Occidental (i.e. Western) history and culture as a whole."[20] This means that

> "[H]uman rights did not develop as a 'natural unfolding' of humanitarian ideas deeply rooted in the cultural and religious traditions of Europe. On the contrary: people in the West, too, had (and still have) to *fight* to have their rights respected. In fighting for their human rights, they faced resistance not only from traditionally privileged groups like the aristocracy or from advocates of an authoritarian State. Anti-liberal currents were also strong among representatives of the churches who feared that the emancipatory spirit of human rights would undermine the moral fabric of Christian society and the hierarchical structure of the clergy."[21]

However, today many religious communities around the world have come to terms with the values of human dignity and human autonomy and now often are ardent defenders or advocates of human rights. Bielefeldt argues that history shows us that it is possible to build a bridge between human rights and

19 E.g. Edmund Burke, in his classic work *Reflections on the Revolution in France* (London: Dent 1910). An example of a recent critique of liberalism (and the individualistic tendencies therein) from the communitarian perspective is the work of Kymlicka (1989). See for a feminist critique of liberalism e.g. Jagger 1993.

20 Bielefeldt 2000, p 96.

21 Ibid.

traditionalist cultures, exactly through clarifying the moral or ethical value orientation of human rights:

> "It is especially the idea of human dignity that can connect human rights with different religious, philosophical, and cultural traditions, because the insight in the unalienable dignity of every human being constitutes both the basic ethical principle of human rights and a central element of the teachings of various religions and philosophies."[22]

TWO FURTHER PREREQUISITES FOR THE DEVELOPMENT OF INTERNATIONAL HUMAN RIGHTS STANDARDS

The coming into being of international legal human rights standards, as we know them today, would have been inconceivable without two important additional developments. First, it had to become accepted that there are boundaries to State sovereignty with regard to how a State treats its own citizens or any other persons who happen to live on its territory; secondly, it also had to become accepted that States could hold each other accountable not only for their own bad or oppressive behaviour towards their inhabitants (i.e. in vertical relationships), but also for the bad or oppressive behaviour of citizens among themselves (i.e. in horizontal relationships).

Limiting State sovereignty in domestic affairs

The idea that a State can give up part of its sovereign powers (or even part of its territory) by means of concluding contracts with other sovereign States (i.e. by means of covenants or treaties) is as old as international law itself. However, until less than a hundred years ago, this did not include accepting interference by other States with affairs that were considered to be strictly *internal* or *domestic*. States were deemed to be absolutely sovereign as to how they treated their own citizens. Signing up to UN (and subsequently, regional) Covenants, Conventions or Treaties in which it was agreed that States parties would respect certain fundamental human rights of their citizens, was a revolutionary step in that regard. From then on, States could hold each other accountable under international law for violations of the rights that were guaranteed under these treaties.

Normally, a treaty between two States parties does not create rights or obligations for third parties (be it other countries, international organisations or individuals).

---

22 Bielefeldt 2000, p 116. See also para. 4.3, where we discuss the desirability of finding a common moral language.

By signing a human rights treaty the State party promises, directly to other States but also indirectly to its own citizens, to respect human rights. In that way, international human rights law regulates rights and freedoms of individual citizens vis-à-vis their own State. As a consequence of the existence of international human rights law individuals now may claim certain rights under treaties that were conducted between sovereign States. Instead of *objects* of international law, individuals have become recognised as *subjects* of international law, i.e. as independent bearers of rights and duties that exist in such law.

State's accountability for human rights violations in horizontal relationships

The final step taken was that it became conceivable that States could also be held accountable for human rights violations in horizontal relationships between citizens or private organisations. This means violations of which the perpetrators are not State officials, but are non-state actors who are present in that particular State. Under international human rights law, States have a positive duty to protect all citizens and other inhabitants from violation of their human rights by other persons or private organisations. This is of particular importance for the protection of women's human rights. Many instances of discrimination against women, or of violence against women, take place in the private sphere. In addition, many forms of discrimination against women are upheld or defended by private organisations, like social and cultural associations and churches or other religious organisations. For this State accountability, the concept of 'due diligence' has been developed in international human rights theory: States have a positive duty to do their utmost best to ensure that no human rights violations by non-state actors take place.[23] This includes the obligation to ensure that such organisations or private persons stop using culture as an excuse to deny women the full enjoyment of their human rights.[24]

THE LEGAL STATURE OF HUMAN RIGHTS

Over the last sixty years most States have come to believe that human rights are related to peace and security and that they have responsibilities to protect their own people and victims elsewhere. They have actually developed a sense of obligation in this respect and have become part of the international human

---

23 See with respect to Violence Against Women and the due diligence principle the Report of the Special Rapporteur on VAW, 'The due diligence standard as a tool for the elimination of violence against women'; 20 January 2006, UN Doc. E/CN.4/2006/61; and Benniger-Budel 2008.

24 The CEDAW Committee, in its Concluding Observations, gives many examples of such obligations. See para. 2.4 and Holtmaat 2011.

rights evolution.[25] Belonging to a community of 'United Nations', individual States for a large part have become to conceive of themselves as being bound by a common set of rules.[26] Human rights norms have become communicative reference points in international society. Gradually, the moral and ethical value of all human being's equality in dignity and rights has evolved into an extensive body of international treaties, which determine the *legal* stature of human rights. It means that States have mutually agreed to give up part of their sovereignty in this respect and are willing to let themselves be supervised by international organisations or supervising bodies, international courts, et cetera.

In international legal theory, it is clarified that States parties have the general duty to implement human rights standards 'in good faith' and with 'due diligence', that they are obliged to take 'all appropriate measures', and to do so 'without delay'. Under international human rights law, States parties have a duty to *respect*, to *protect*, to *fulfil* and to *promote* these standards in their own country and among their citizens.[27] This entitles governments of States to hold other States parties accountable when these obligations are not respected. Although it is accepted that many human rights standards need a gradual implementation,[28] States parties to international human rights treaties are not allowed to be completely passive, or to excuse themselves with reference to their economic, social or cultural situation. Most importantly, the legal stature of human rights implies that a State party to an international human rights treaty cannot invoke provisions of its domestic law as a justification for a failure to perform its duties under international law.[29] In the ideal situation, a State not only is willing to draw up and submit a report on its internal affairs and to discuss this report with international supervising bodies, but is also willing to commit itself to the observations or comments of such bodies, including a judgement in an individual complaint procedure or a judgement of an international court in this area (such as the European Court of Human Rights). Regretfully, up to date not all States comply to this ideal.[30]

---

25 Lauren 2007, p 326.

26 Clark 2001, p 28–30.

27 See e.g. Sepúlveda 2003, in particular Chapter 5, and Cook & Cusack 2010, p 76–84.

28 This is especially true of social, economic and cultural rights. Basic political and civil rights (as the right to vote or the right not to be tortured) have to be implemented immediately. It is a point for discussion whether the right to non-discrimination is 'immediate'. As far as States parties' own actions are concerned, one could argue that there is no reason for any delay, while the eradication of all forms of discrimination in the wider society may take more time.

29 See also para. 2.4, where we discuss that State parties to CEDAW often argue that under their Constitution particular religious or customary laws have a '*status aparte*', i.e. are exempted from the application of (Constitutional) equality norms.

30 A sad example is the way in which the Dutch Government refused to follow up on CEDAW-Committee's recommendations to take action against a fundamentalist Christian political party that denied women access to party membership and political representation in elected bodies. See Boerefijn 2010.

INTERNATIONAL PRESSURE TO IMPLEMENT HUMAN RIGHTS

The idea that States are accountable for human rights violations on the international level was gradually accepted by most national governments (which is exemplified by the fact that most of them have ratified the main Human Rights Treaties at the UN level and at the regional level). However, this does not mean that in practice they easily accept interference by other States with their domestic or internal affairs. This becomes clear from the resistance that *Special Rapporteurs* (e.g. on Torture or on Violence Against Women) encounter when they want to inspect a country's policies and practices. Or from the fact that sometimes only after a lot of international pressure States are willing to implement international human rights standards. Several mechanisms may contribute to implementation of international human rights standards at the national level: processes of *coercion* (externally imposed with sanctions and incentives), *persuasion* (if States are open and accept and internalise norms) and *acculturation* (which may lead to conformity, but may easily be reversed when external and internal pressure stops).[31] Pressure through diplomatic channels and political pressure (including 'silent diplomacy'), and via confrontation at the multinational level have appeared to be effective. It causes isolation and 'a mobilisation of shame', which may pressure a State party into a certain degree of implementation of human rights standards at the national level.

THE ROLE OF NGOS

The development of international human rights law would not have been possible without the persistent lobby and advocacy of non-governmental organisations (NGOs). Although the Universal Declaration was adopted in 1948, until the early 1960's the community of nations exhibited almost no willingness to hold individual States accountable for human rights violations. Since then, much has changed due to the consistent approach of human rights NGOs, focussing on the adoption and application of fundamental human rights norms. In particular Amnesty International, founded in 1961, played a crucial role in this respect. Its particular attributes have lent legitimacy to this organisation in the international system and have enabled it to serve as a model for other NGOs.[32] Human rights NGOs have thus succeeded to stretch the limits of NGO participation and influence at the United Nations' institutional bodies. Collectively, NGOs have

---

31 See Avdeyeva 2007 and Hawkins 2004.

32 See Clark 2001, Chapter 1, who explains that this organisation holds three unique attributes: loyalty to the moral principle of human rights; a position of disinterested and autonomous 'third party' actor in the international system; and expertise and large amounts of specific information.

acquired broad experience, using transnational pressure from citizens to affect norms of government practice in varying areas of economic, social, political and cultural life.

Equally important is the role of local (often grass root) NGOs that observe and report human rights violations. Their contribution is all the more crucial because not only State actors may violate human rights, but also individuals and private organisations. Transposition of international human rights standards into local practices and beliefs requires a continuous effort to inform and educate people about their human rights. National and local NGOs are the most important 'transmitters' in this respect. Besides, local NGOs have a close connection to local customs, beliefs or traditions, and are able to build bridges between local and universal normative systems. Therefore, one of the important contributions that such organisations can make, is that they may make it possible to develop a common value based language that may facilitate a real dialogue about the implementation of women's human rights.[33]

HUMAN RIGHTS – IDEA AND PROJECT

Taking a closer look at what people actually mean when they talk about human rights, reveals that we can distinguish between the *human rights idea* (i.e. the moral principle of the equal dignity and rights of all human beings) and the *human rights project* (embodied in various legal documents and promoted by contemporary political institutions).[34] Both are crucial for the realisation of women's human rights: the moral principle of human equality needs to be broadly accepted in society, but also needs to be codified in international and national law and regulations and in case law. Human rights do not only exist as ideas or ideals and/or as legal norms, but they have to be realised all the time. Often, the moral or cultural legitimisation of human rights is lacking, and/or their legal construction and their implementation in national legislation, policies and practices is weak.

As for the moral aspect, we need to be aware of the fact that for a lot of people the basic idea of human equality is still a counter intuitive idea. Human equality is an extraordinary difficult idea or ideal that does not easily circulate among people. It is much easier to take it that we are all different from each other and that people(s) who are not 'like us' are in some way a threat. Human beings are constructing differences between themselves all the time – from playing fields to

33 See also para. 4.3, where we discuss the necessity of finding a common moral language, based on already existing norms or values within local communities.

34 See De Gaay Fortman 1997.

political parties, sometimes leading to a strong and hostile feeling of 'us' and 'them'.[35] The basic idea of human equality thus encounters a lot of resistance.

For human rights to be fully realised in law and in practice, they need both legal and cultural legitimisation. Berta Hernández Truyol calls the latter the symbolic validation of (new) rules and laws, including the human rights norms of equality in rights and in dignity.[36] She remarks that religion, tradition and culture can supply this kind of validation. However, in large parts of the world especially the norm of equality between men and women until now has a weak symbolic validation. It is a relatively young concept that most people, also in the Western world, have not yet fully internalised. In Chapter 3, where we discuss the construction of gender and unequal gender relations, it becomes clear how deeply the idea that men and women are not equal but different is engraved in our minds, often on the subconscious level. The human rights project, therefore, will never succeed when it does not (also) take this orientation towards difference instead of (solely) equality into account.[37]

THE CONTINUED POLITICAL PROFILE OF HUMAN RIGHTS

Above we sketched that the (r)evolution of the coming into being of human rights was connected to a lot of severe political struggles at the national and the international level. This struggle has not yet come to an end. Human rights have always been and continue to be critical of existing social, economic, cultural and legal norms and structures in a given society. As such human rights advocates are part of a political struggle over maintaining or subverting existing power relations.[38] Often, human rights work as an eye opener in the sense that they make people aware that certain oppressive conditions of life are not natural (or predestined or eternal) and should/could be changed.[39] They are critical of any situation that denies people the full enjoyment of all of their internationally

35 Especially when such differences are constructed along the lines of such characteristics as race, ethnicity, nationality, sex, sexual orientation, they may become discriminatory. See the lists of non-discrimination grounds in various international human rights treaties, like e.g. in Article 26 ICCPR or Article 14 ECHR.

36 Hernández-Truyol 2002, p 148 ff.

37 Another argument, made in this book, is that human rights advocates and lawyers should not only focus on equality, as the central human rights value, but should also highlight the central place of human dignity.

38 Bielefeldt 2000, p 101, states that "the history of human rights in the West gives us an *example* – not the paradigm per se, but merely an example – of the various obstacles, misunderstandings, learning processes, achievements, and failures in the long-standing struggle for human rights."

39 See for a most interesting theoretical discussions of human rights' moral power Winston 2007 and Peters 1983. The necessity of finding 'eye openers' is discussed in more detail in para. 3.2, where we deal with the invisibility of gender stereotypes.

guaranteed human rights and offer a program of reform.[40] Today, now that human rights have become part of the global vernacular, the revolutionary meaning of human rights is not so apparent anymore. But existing power relations and human rights are often at odds with one another; therefore, ruling powers will seek ways to neglect or obstruct implementation of human rights standards when any such implementation would threaten their position. Whenever certain individuals or groups that thus far have been marginalised or excluded, claim that their equal human rights should be respected too, they run against vested interests, and efforts will be made to retain the status quo. For that reason human rights were and will continue to be politically contested. Human rights, in other words, are not (yet) a quiet possession, but need to be made real time and again in each and every political and legal system on the globe. This is certainly true as far as women's human rights are concerned.

2.2 THE HUMAN RIGHTS OF WOMEN AS LAID DOWN IN CEDAW

THE ADOPTION OF A UN CONVENTION CONFIRMING WOMEN'S HUMAN RIGHTS

The development of the (legal) concept of citizenship rights and human rights did not guarantee that women (as well as slaves, children, non-white persons, colonised people, persons with disabilities, and other 'minorities') gained access to these rights from the very beginning. On the contrary, for a long time these human beings were considered not to be rational and autonomous individuals who could and should be able to freely decide about their own course of life. Women, most importantly, under most national Constitutions that were adopted after the 18th Century Revolutions and in the thereafter established new nation States, were not considered as full citizens with a complete set of citizenship rights and civil rights. Until far into the 20th century – including in the most economically and socially developed Western States – women lacked such basic rights as the right to vote and the right to own property or the handling of such property, or the right to give her nationality to her children. Especially married women had the status of a person incapable of making autonomous decisions

40 See e.g. Article 1 CEDAW, where discrimination is defined as "any distinction, exclusion or restriction made on the basis of sex which has the effect or purpose of impairing or nullifying the recognition, enjoyment or exercise by women (...) of human rights and fundamental freedoms in the political, economic, social, cultural, civil or any other field." Similar definitions can be found in Article 1 ICERD and Article 1 ICRPD. (See for the full text of this definition, para. 2.2).

about her own affairs in life. In many legal systems they were equated with young children and/or with mentally disabled persons.[41]

This situation did not go unnoticed by the United Nations. After the adoption of the Universal Declaration in 1948 and the two main human rights treaties (ICCPR and ICESCR) at the beginning of the 1960's, it was deemed necessary to add an international treaty on the human right of women not to be discriminated against.[42] The UN Convention on the Elimination of All Forms of Discrimination Against Women (CEDAW) was adopted in 1979 and entered into force in 1981.[43] The Convention is now (AD 2010) ratified by 186 States.[44] This shows that States have wished to visibly join the universal consensus on the importance of women's human rights. At the same time however, when it comes to actual implementation of the principle of women's equality, many States prefer a large degree of national discretionary power to act in accordance with their own (traditional) ideas about the nature of the relationships between the two sexes. This is apparent from the fact that CEDAW is also the human rights Convention where reservations to certain provisions were most frequently made.[45]

THE CEDAW COMMITTEE

The Committee on the Elimination of Discrimination Against Women is the supervisory body of the Convention, tasked with monitoring the implementation of the treaty provisions by the States parties. The Committee is comprised of 23 independent experts, elected from among nationals of the States parties. All States parties to CEDAW are obliged to report periodically to this Committee on their progress made in the implementation of the convention.[46] In the subsequent *constructive dialogue* between the Committee and a delegation of the State party

---

41 In The Netherlands it took until 1956 for married women to gain full legal capacity in civil law. In some Swiss Cantons, women got the right to vote only in the 1980s.

42 For a description of the political and legal process of the adoption of CEDAW see Rehof 1993.

43 The efforts to put women's human rights on the agenda of international co-operation has not ended with the adoption of CEDAW, on the contrary. The issue re-appears in e.g. the 4 World Conferences on Women, in the 1993 Vienna World Conference on Human Rights and in many other international Conferences and UN meetings, leading to numerous Resolutions and Declarations in this area. In this book, we concentrate on CEDAW, being the core global *legal* document in this area.

44 All information on CEDAW can be found at: www.un.org/womenwatch/daw/cedaw/ (last accessed on July 20, 2010). See for an extensive discussion of the work of the Committee Schöpp-Schilling & Flinterman 2007.

45 Reservations to Article 2 (the right to equality in and before the law) and Article 16 (the right to equality in family matters) are most frequent. See Flinterman 2010.

46 The first report needs to be submitted within one year after the entry into force of the convention for the State concerned; thereafter they need to report every four year (Article 18 CEDAW).

concerned, these reports are being discussed. The Committee exemplifies how the treaty provisions need to be interpreted and what this means for the State's policies.

In response to this dialogue, the Committee draws up *Concluding Observations* (or *Concluding Comments*)[47] noting positive points, but also points of concern, coupled with recommendations.[48] The Committee avoids bluntly condemning States' practices but rather offers advice as to how to improve the situation.[49] The *Concluding Observations* are not legally binding, but CEDAW States parties are expected to follow up on the Committee's recommendations. Besides, the Committee issues *General Recommendations*, clarifying the interpretation of treaty provisions and thus the obligations for States parties, in light of certain economic, political and social developments.

Civil society organisations may provide the Committee with so-called shadow reports, containing supplementary information and critical comments to the official Government's report. Notably, when seeking to clarify issues of culture and putting the Government's report in context, the additional information is of crucial importance. It is worth noting that all CEDAW documents, including the shadow reports, are public documents and can be consulted on the internet.[50] This enables observers to have a good picture of the challenges for each State party and of the Committee's concerns and comments.

Besides this general review procedure, the Committee has the task to receive and consider complaints sent by individuals under CEDAW's Optional Protocol.[51] In addition, Article 8 of the Optional Protocol grants the Committee the right to examine, on its own motion, reliable information indicating grave or systematic violations of women's human rights and transmit its findings and recommendations to the State Party concerned. The Committee for the first time

---

47 Concluding Observations (CO's) until 2008 (41st Session) can be found at www.un.org/womenwatch/daw/cedaw; from then onwards, they are published on www2.ohchr.org/english/bodies/cedaw/index.htm (last accessed on July 20, 2010). In our footnotes we have cited the official UN Documents (UN Doc.A/...) whenever the CEDAW CO's are only included in the annual UN reports. From 2005 onwards, CEDAW CO's have identifiable numbers and will be cited as such.

48 In this book we have included quite a lot of references to CEDAW CO's; this enables readers to get a better understanding of how the Committee deals with the issue of women's human rights and culture.

49 According to Cees Flinterman, Dutch member of the CEDAW Committee, the Committee does not so much speaks of having observed *violations* of CEDAW, but will more diplomatically establish incompatibility with, or being at odds with or not in full compliance with the treaty obligations (personal comment, September 2009).

50 To be downloaded from www2.ohchr.org/english/bodies/cedaw/index.htm (last accessed on July 20, 2010).

51 Adopted on 6 October 1999, and entered into force on 22 December 2000.

used this right in the inquiry into the rapes and murders of women in and around Ciudad Juarez in Mexico.[52]

THE SCOPE AND PURPOSE OF CEDAW

Article 1 of the CEDAW Convention provides the definition of discrimination against women:

> "Any distinction, exclusion or restriction made on the basis of sex which has the effect or purpose of impairing or nullifying the recognition, enjoyment or exercise by women, irrespective of their marital status, on a basis of equality of men and women, of human rights and fundamental freedoms in the political, economic, social, cultural, and civil or any other field".

From this definition it appears that the scope of CEDAW is very wide; it covers all spheres of life, including the private sphere.[53] CEDAW explicitly recognises the disadvantaged position of women and awards protection to women exclusively.[54] The words 'distinction, exclusion or restriction' are interpreted broadly by the Committee and by commentators, in order to target *all forms* of discrimination against women. By making a connection between the principle of equality between men and women and women's human rights, the Convention adheres to a human rights based interpretation of the principle of non-discrimination, as opposed to a formal legal approach to this principle, in which a *sex equality* or an *equal treatment norm* prevails.[55] In the human rights approach, discrimination of women is seen as an instance of their *oppression*, which, according to Iris Marion Young, can take at least five different forms. What women face, according to Young, is *oppression*, i.e. a mixture of exploitation, marginalisation, powerlessness, cultural imperialism and violence.[56] This means that not only (sexual) harassment, violence against women, sexist hate speech, or unequal treatment on the ground of sex should be ruled out, but also more hidden or indirect forms of discrimination. This includes structural discrimination that is rooted in culture.

52 Report on Mexico, CEDAW/C/2005/OP.8/Mexico, 27 January 2005.

53 This is concluded from the fact that Article 2 contains the obligation to put an end to all discrimination, even when it occurs in horizontal relationships.

54 This differs from neutral or symmetrical anti-discrimination provisions in many national constitutions and equal treatment laws, and in e.g. European law, where it unequal treatment on the ground of (either male or female) *sex* is prohibited. See Holtmaat & Tobler 2005.

55 Formal equality, in its purest form, is disconnected from the question which of he sexes is structurally being oppressed or suffers from general societal disadvantages. It applies the equal treatment norm in a symmetrical way. See Holtmaat & Tobler 2005 for a comparative analysis of mainstream (EU) sex equality law and CEDAW.

56 Young 1990, p 40. See also Winston 2007, who sees organising countervailing powers to *oppression* as the main objective of human rights.

Articles 2–5 of CEDAW cover the general obligations for States parties. They contain norms to be regarded on their own merits, but they are also indicative to the interpretation and implementation of all other substantive Articles in the Convention. Articles 6 to 16 specify a number of fields in which the States parties need to take appropriate measures, such as trafficking in women (Article 6), participation in political life and public offices (Articles 7–8), the right to nationality (Article 9), the equal right to education (Article 10) to work and remuneration (Article 11), to health care (Article 12), to social benefits (Article 13), and equality in civil law (Article 15) and in marriage and family relations (Article 16). Special attention is given to the position of rural women (Article 14).

In General Recommendation 25, the Committee has clarified that the object and purpose of the Convention is:

1. to ensure full equality of women before the law and protection against discrimination in the public as well as the private sphere (formal equality),
2. to improve the de facto position of women (substantive equality), and
3. to address prevailing gender relations and the persistence of gender-based stereotypes (transformative equality).[57]

THREE DIMENSIONS OF EQUALITY AND THREE STRATEGIES FOR COMBATING DISCRIMINATION AGAINST WOMEN

This threefold object and purpose of the Convention corresponds to a threefold interpretation of the fundamental principle of equality. To begin with, Article 2 of the Convention makes it unambiguously clear that women do indeed have equal rights under the law and should not be treated differently purely because they are a woman. This principle is repeated in many Articles that cover specific areas, like for example Articles 7–8 on political life and public offices, Articles 11–13 on social and health rights and Articles 15 and 16 on civil rights and family rights. This *principle of formal equality* is one of the core principles of any democratic legal order.[58]

In addition, the Convention in its Articles 3, 4 and 24 makes it clear that all appropriate measures need to be taken in order to achieve women's *de facto*

57 CEDAW GR 25, paras 6 and 7.

58 This principle (also sometimes called the principle of legality as such!) means that any categorisation between citizens that are subjects of the law should reflect a *real* and *relevant* difference between them. The principle of formal equality between the sexes means that sex is seen as an irrelevant difference, unless it is proven otherwise. See also para. 4.3.

equality with men. This means that sometimes additional temporary special measures are necessary, a concept which is elaborated in Article 4(1).[59] In that way, the Convention includes the *principle of substantive equality.* It means that CEDAW acknowledges that individual people through place of birth, mental and physical capacities, wealth, development of the country, discrimination, and a whole range of other (including cultural) causes, in fact have very different positions and possibilities in life. Although equal in moral terms, or in terms of their fundamental human rights, in real life people are very different from each other, also in terms of opportunities to make something of their life. Women, in many cultures around the world are in a position of inequality and severe oppression, not only because of their physical or biological difference from men, but also because of persistent discrimination against them. The Convention requires that women be given an equal starting point and that they be empowered by an enabling environment to achieve *de facto* equality. For this reason the Committee calls for the urgent introduction of temporary special measures.[60]

The Convention's third objective of addressing prevailing gender relations and the persistence of gender-based stereotypes is based on Article 5.[61] According to the Committee this Article means that the Convention acknowledges that these phenomena "(…) affect women not only through individual acts by individuals but also in law, and legal and societal structures and institutions."[62] Through the inclusion of this provision, the Convention also addresses the *systemic and structural inequality* of women, and – in order to overcome the structural discrimination that results from that inequality – calls for *transformative equality.*[63]

Transformative equality, or 'equality as transformation', aims at changing society in such a way that those features of existing culture and of legal, social and economic structures that obstruct the equality and human dignity of women are subjected to fundamental change. "On the basis of this transformative view of equality, States parties are required to undertake a social re-ordering of their political economy, and the cultural valuations ascribed to men and women."[64]

---

59 Boerefijn et al 2003.

60 CEDAW GR 25, para. 8. See also Boerefijn et al 2003.

61 See the text of this Article in the next sub-paragraph.

62 CEDAW GR 25, para. 7. See also e.g. CO Luxembourg, UN Doc.A/55/38, 22nd Session (2000) para. 404.

63 Fredman 2003, p 116. See also Otto 1997, speaking of transformative human rights, and Cornell 1993. The latter defines 'transformative' as having two meanings. First "change, radical enough to so dramatically restructure any system – political, legal or social – that the 'identity' of the system is itself altered. The second meaning, (…) turns to the question of what kind of individuals we would have to become in order to open ourselves to new worlds." (As cited by Otto 1997, p 3, fn 12.).

64 Cusack & Cook 2009, p 207. See also Cook & Cusack 2010, p 5.

This requirement has become an international *legal obligation* of States parties, through Article 5 CEDAW that requires a modification of social and cultural patterns of conduct and family education about the sharing of family responsibilities between the parents.[65] Article 5 therefore embodies what may also be phrased as the *principle of cultural change*.[66] The Committee has adopted the principle of transformative equality in 2004, when it stated that measures must be taken "towards a real transformation of opportunities, institutions and systems so that they are no longer grounded in historically determined male paradigms of power and life patterns."[67]

These three approaches to the fundamental principle of equality should not be seen as competing ways of conceptualising the basic norm of equality. In fact, they are complementary to each other. As the Convention makes clear, they should be seen as the basis for a *simultaneously* applied (holistic) approach to combating discrimination against women. For that purpose, three different strategies should be applied. First, there needs to be a strategy of giving individual people a *right* to equal treatment before and in the law (the *Individual Rights Strategy*). This means that national constitutions should contain a non-discrimination clause, and that national equal treatment legislation should be in place, giving women the effective legal right to contest any case of discrimination in court and to be supported with legal aid in that respect. Secondly, governments should develop a strategy of social support to those who have least opportunities to lead a meaningful life as a human being, for example to those who are disabled or poor, and/or who are discriminated against on the ground of sex (a *Social Support Strategy*).[68] Such strategies could include temporary special measures, or pro-active programmes to overcome the consequences of past and present discrimination. Thirdly, governments should embark on a strategy to take away the structural causes of any such discrimination through a process of social and cultural change (*Strategy of Social and Cultural Change*).[69]

---

65 Fredman 2003, p 116; Van Maarseveen 1987, p 75.

66 This analysis of Article 5 was first elaborated in the work of a Commission of independent legal experts, installed by the Dutch government, which did in-depth study into the nature and scope of CEDAW. See Groenman et al. 1997. Rikki Holtmaat was a member of this Commission. The government subscribed to the Commission's interpretation, which was reported to the Committee in the 3rd CEDAW Country Report of the Netherlands in 2000. The Committee appreciated this analysis. See CO The Netherlands, UN Doc.A/56/38, 25th Session (2001) para. 196. The Groenman Commission based itself upon the historical background and a textual analysis of Article 5, on Concluding Observations of the Committee, and on *inter alia* studies of Van Maarseveen 1987, Heringa, Hes & Lijnzaad 1994, and Hes & Van Vleuten 1996.

67 CEDAW GR 25, para. 10.

68 Social support should be targeted to specific groups of women that are in a particular vulnerable position. Therefore, it is important to recognise that women may become the victim of intersectional or multiple discrimination. See also para. 3.2.

69 See e.g. Groenman et al 1997, Holtmaat 2002(a) and Holtmaat 2004.

2.3 ARTICLE 5 CEDAW

ARTICLE 5 CEDAW AS A CORE OBLIGATION TO END DISCRIMINATION AGAINST WOMEN

For the purpose of this book, the third objective of CEDAW has special relevance because it addresses prevailing gender relations and the persistence of gender-based stereotypes, which means that it concerns culture.[70] The CEDAW Committee holds that this third objective is expressed in particular in Article 5, which provides that

> "States parties shall take all appropriate measures
> a) To modify the social and cultural patterns of conduct of men and women, with a view to achieving the elimination of prejudices and customary and all other practices which are based on the idea of the inferiority or the superiority of either of the sexes or on stereotyped roles for men and women;
> b) To ensure that family education includes a proper understanding of maternity as a social function and the recognition of the common responsibility of men and women in the upbringing and development of their children, it being understood that the interest of the children is the primordial consideration in all cases."

Article 5 is based on the Preamble where the drafters of the Convention have stressed the fact that it is of great importance to see maternity as a positive value, instead of as a cause for discrimination against women.[71] The drafters were fully aware that a change in the traditional role of men as well as the role of women in society and in the family is needed to achieve full equality between men and women.[72] Article 5 CEDAW speaks of the idea of inferiority or superiority of either of the sexes. With that phrase, CEDAW expresses a fundamental insight in the persistent unequal nature of gender relations.

While subsection (a) of Article 5 obliges States parties to eliminate all harmful practices that are based on the idea of the inferiority or the superiority of either of the sexes or on stereotyped roles for men and women, subsection (b) concerns the fact that in most cultures and traditions in the world women are seen as primary carers of their children and relatives, while at the same time they are

---

70 See also para. 3.2 for the relationship between gender (stereotypes) and culture.

71 The drafters took care to distinguish between maternity (biological) and motherhood (social). See Holtmaat 2011 (forthcoming). Maternity is also protected in Articles 4(2) and 11(2). The Committee acknowledges that protection of motherhood may easily lead to regulations that are oppressive for women. See below, in this paragraph.

72 CEDAW Preamble, paras 13 and 14. Article 5 often is read in conjunction with Article 2(f), which obliges States parties that appropriate measures, including legislation, should be used to modify and abolish existing laws, regulations, customs and practices which constitute discrimination against women.

deprived of many of their rights under the guise that women's proper role is in the family.[73] Article 5 provides that negative and damaging traditional, cultural or religious beliefs, ideas, rules and practices concerning women's so-called natural or predestined role in private and public life, should be replaced by a positive appreciation of women's contribution to social life and by a practice of sharing parental roles by men and women. Both parts of Article 5 thus are two sides of the same coin. Consequently, the Article instructs States parties to adopt a comprehensive and effective strategy to combat discrimination against women. Briefly summarised, Article 5 CEDAW contains the obligation, to which States parties to the Convention have committed themselves, *to modify gender stereotypes and fixed parental gender roles in order to realise full equality of women and men.*[74]

In terms of Iris Marion Young's description of various forms of oppression of women, as discussed above, Article 5 CEDAW can be seen as a legal norm that addresses in particular women's marginalisation and cultural imperialism. The inclusion of this provision in the Convention makes it possible to read the non-discrimination principle, that is laid down in the Convention, as a general human rights norm that addresses *all* the different forms that discrimination against women can take, including women's formal and substantive inequality in laws and public policies, and in all other (public and private) institutions and practices, harassment, violence and stigmatisation, prejudice, ideas about their inferiority and gender stereotyping.

THE IMPORTANCE OF ARTICLE 5 ACCORDING TO THE COMMITTEE

Gender stereotypes and fixed parental gender roles can be related to discrimination against women in two ways. First, they can be seen as *causing discrimination* against women. Second, they can also be seen as being *discriminatory in themselves*. According to the Committee, both perspectives are possible, as is apparent form the following standard consideration in many Concluding Observations:

> "The Committee continues to be concerned about the persistence of patriarchal attitudes and deep-rooted stereotypes regarding the role and responsibilities of men and women in society, *which discriminate against women*. The Committee is also concerned that the preservation of negative cultural practices and traditional attitudes *serves to perpetuate women's subordination* in the family and society and

[73] Raday 2007, p 74.

[74] See also Holtmaat 2011.

constitutes a serious obstacle to women's enjoyment of their fundamental rights." [Italics added.][75]

The Committee has further elaborated on the relationship between culture and discrimination of women in many Concluding Observations[76], as well as in a number of General Recommendations, for example such as the one on Article 7 (political rights):

> "In all nations, the most significant factors inhibiting women's ability to participate in public life have been the cultural framework of values and religious beliefs, the lack of services and men's failure to share the tasks associated with the organization of the household and with the care and raising of children. In all nations, cultural traditions and religious beliefs have played a part in confining women to the private spheres of activity and excluding them from active participation in public life."[77]

The Committee time and again has explained that gender stereotypes and fixed parental gender roles have a negative impact on *all* of women's human rights, as guaranteed under the Convention:

> "The Committee expresses a general concern about the persistence of discriminatory stereotypes and cultural practices and traditions of a patriarchal nature relating to the roles and responsibilities of women and men in the family and in society, as they constitute serious obstacles to women's educational and professional prospects and the enjoyment of their human rights and contribute to the persistence of violence against women."[78]

States parties to CEDAW are under an obligation to eliminate *all forms* of discrimination against women and to protect the victims of such discrimination, irrespective of whether the perpetrator is a State official or a private party (non-state actor). This includes discrimination that is based on or vested in a particular culture. This means that not only should States parties decline any appeal to culture by any State or private actors who violate women's human rights, but that they should also actively engage in combating instances of discrimination

---

75 CO Burundi, CEDAW/C/BDI/CO/4 (2008) para. 17.

76 The Committee uses various terms to express the nature of the relationship between gender stereotyping and discriminating against women. For example it states that stereotypes "*constitute barriers* to..." (CO Cook Islands, CEDAW/C/COK/CO/1 (2007) para. 28), that they "constitute the most *serious obstacles* to ..." (CO Cyprus, UN Doc.A/51/38, 15th Session (1996) para. 45), or that they "*present impediments* to ... and *are a root cause* of..." (CO New Zealand, CEDAW/C/NZL/CO/6 (2007) para. 22.) The fact that stereotypes as such discriminate against women is also being stressed in many Concluding Observations; see e.g. CO Guinea, CEDAW/C/EST/GIN/CO/6 (2007) para. 23.

77 CEDAW GR 23, para. 10. See Also CEDAW GR 21, para. 41 on the position of women in family relationships.

78 CO Mozambique, CEDAW/C/MOZ/CO/2 (2007) paras 20, 21. See for a list of similar references Koukoulis-Spiliotopoulos 2008, p 420, footnote 33.

against women that are based on gender stereotypes and fixed parental gender roles.[79]

THE VALUE BASIS OF ARTICLE 5

In order to fully understand the normative impact of Article 5 CEDAW, it should be recollected that human rights in general are based on the idea of rational and autonomous human beings that have inalienable rights (see para. 2.1). Contrary to that idea, gender stereotypes are social, legal and cultural constructions of firm (closed and opposite) categories of male and female human beings, on the basis of which a set of fixed characteristics are attributed to all of those who are placed within either of these two categories.[80] People are expected to behave 'normally', i.e. in accordance with descriptive and prescriptive stereotypes about what is seen as 'proper' male or female behaviour. For example, men are expected to be breadwinners, women are expected to stay at home and take care of the children. Such stereotypes and fixed parental gender roles, especially when they are embedded or inscribed in the society's most important public institutions, laws, social and cultural practices and religious beliefs, result in a deprivation of control over people's own lives. To stay with the example: in such a society it is extremely difficult for a man to stay at home to take care of the children and for a woman to go out for paid work.[81]

Gender stereotypes and fixed parental gender roles, in other words, run against the very basic idea on which human rights is founded: the capacity of each human being to take rational and autonomous decisions about his or her own course of life. In fact, when these stereotypes are linked to *traditional or customary ideas about the inferiority or superiority of either of the sexes* they will inevitably lead to sustaining structural gender inequality. The *social and cultural patterns of conduct* and *stereotyped roles* which are addressed by Article 5 CEDAW, which are based on *prejudice* and on *customary and other practices*, deny individual women the right to full personhood. It denies them the possibility to be a person in their own right and to utilise all of their human

79 The Committee is sometimes accused of 'enculturing' women's inequality, that is: seeing the causes thereof solely in terms of culture, not in terms of for example economic oppression and exploitation (e.g. by the West or by capitalist companies), or of internal and external military conflicts. See e.g. Merry 2003 Polar, where she states that: "While this attribution of cultural factors is undoubtedly accurate, again the responsibility is located in the domain of beliefs and values to the exclusion of political, economic, or structural factors."

80 See also para. 3.2.

81 See Mackie & LeJeune 2009 for an extensive discussion of the difficulties that individual people experience when they want to 'rebel' against social norms.

capacities and capabilities in order to lead a meaningful life as a human being.[82] Gender stereotypes and fixed parental gender roles, therefore, not only deny women the right to be respectfully treated as an equal and dignified human being. They also deny women the freedom to live their lives according to their own choice and convictions about their personal and unique contribution to sustaining and developing humanity.

Women and men have a fundamental right not to be confined to culturally defined constructions of femininity or masculinity, or to pre-fixed (and fixated) female and male parental roles that are entrenched in their culture, as well as in the main social and legal institutions or organisations of society.[83] The CEDAW Committee has made it clear that a correct implementation of the Convention requires "the recognition that women can have various roles in society, not only the important role of mother and wife, exclusively responsible for children and the family, but also as an individual person and actor in her community and in the society in general."[84] All human being are equal and have equal rights and deserve equal respect for their human dignity, but that at the same time they may have very *diverse* ideas and wishes about what they actually want to do with their lives.[85] Therefore, the principles of individual autonomy and diversity are crucial for a correct understanding of the content and scope of Article 5 and of the Convention as a whole.[86]

These principles similarly underlie all anti-discrimination clauses in international human rights law and in national constitutions, which ban unequal and undignified treatment on the basis of an individual belonging to a certain 'category' or 'class' of human beings. In a South African case it was clarified that

> "[w]hat the Constitution requires is that the law and public institutions acknowledge the variability of human beings and affirm the equal respect and concern that should be shown to all as they are. At the very least, what is statistically normal ceases to be the basis for establishing what is legally normative. (...) What becomes normal in an open society, then, is not an imposed and standardized form of behaviour that

82 Terms used by Hernández-Truyol 2002, p 146, and Nussbaum 2000. The latter discusses in length what from years of cross-cultural discussions appears to be essential to promote the capabilities of each person. On p. 78–80 of her book she provides an open-ended list of the 'central human capabilities', as basis for determining a decent social minimum in a variety of areas. They bear close resemblance to human rights (see also p. 98 ff).

83 Cook & Cusack 2010, p 68.

84 CO Suriname, UN Doc.A/57/38, 27th Session (2002) para. 48. See also CO Uzbekistan, UN Doc.A/56/38, 24th Session (2001) para. 169.

85 Lijnzaad 1994, p 57.

86 See Baer 2010 (refering to Baer 2009), p 75: "Therefore, I suggest employing an understanding of human rights based on equality, liberty and dignity, in a triangulated perspective of recognition."

refuses to acknowledge difference, but the acceptance of the principle of difference itself."[87]

2.4 CEDAW'S COMMITMENT TO CHANGING DISCRIMINATORY CULTURES

The topic of this book is how it may be avoided that discussions about women's human rights and culture end up in a clash between assertions about competing rights. As we have seen above (in para. 2.3), Article 5 CEDAW contains the norm that traditional and oppressive gender norms need to be modified. In this paragraph, we will explain what this norm entails: what kind of cultural practices need to be changed, and what exactly should States do in order to comply with this provision. From this analysis it will appear that in the eyes of the CEDAW Committee the principles of women's equality and non-discrimination clearly prevail when it is established that cultural practices and believes stand in the way of women's full enjoyment of their human rights.

CULTURAL PRACTICES THAT HAVE BEEN ADDRESSED BY THE COMMITTEE

Culture is a very important positive aspect of human life, which deserves the full and effective protection of international human rights instruments. (This will be further discussed in para. 2.5). In fact, in Article 13(c) the Convention itself protects women from discrimination in all aspects of their cultural life. Culture is essential for human life because it forms the basis for individual identity formation and may empower individuals to become full human beings. The Committee has explicitly acknowledged the positive influence that a culture can have in advancing women's human rights, for example where it "noted that culture is a positive vehicle for influencing the advancement of women, and suggested that cultural art forms be used as a vehicle to promote respect for women."[88] Or where it stated that "[g]iven the existence of different ethnic and indigenous groups in Guyana, members wanted to know if they had preserved their cultural roots, because culture could be used as a unifying force in development."[89] The Committee shows (gradually more) sympathy for positive aspects of a given culture and has acknowledged that at some points traditional

---

87 South African Supreme Court 1999 1 SA 6 (CC), *National Coalition for Gay and Lesbian Equality vs Ministry of Justice*, para. 143, as quoted by Bonthuys & Albertyn 2007, p 28.

88 CO Antigua and Barbuda, UN Doc.A/52/38, 17th Session (1997) para. 270.

89 CO Guyana, UN Doc.A/49/38, 13th Session (1994) para. 101.

or religious values can contribute in a positive way in the process of improving women's human rights.[90]

Nevertheless, most of the time such considerations are followed by the Committee's serious concerns about the negative impact that the same culture may have on women's human rights: "While acknowledging that several traditional perceptions and practices in Bhutan favour women, including with regard to inheritance, the Committee remains concerned that some traditions and stereotyped views in the country may be discriminatory of women and girls, and perpetuate sex-specific roles and responsibilities in some spheres of life."[91] Or: "While noting the value of the cultural heritage of Cambodia, the Committee is concerned about strong gender-role stereotyping, in particular that reflected in the traditional code of conduct known as *chbab srey*, which legitimizes discrimination against women and impedes women's full enjoyment of their human rights and the achievement of equality between men and women in Cambodian society."[92]

From these last quotes it becomes clear that, however important it may be, culture can also function as an underlying cause of discrimination against women or may be discriminatory in itself. Culture may constitute an important obstacle to equality and dignity of women in the private sphere, as well as in public and political life. The Committee acknowledges that *all* human societies suffer from gender stereotypes and fixed parental gender roles, Western and non-Western societies alike. However, as far as the application of the two parts of Article 5 is concerned a certain division of the world can be observed.[93] The Committee most often refers to harmful practices that result from gender stereotyping in relation to culture in the context of Article 5(a) when it discusses the situation of women in third world and/or developing countries. It mainly discusses the damaging effects of fixed parental gender roles and the correct implementation of Article 5(b) with respect to former communist countries and Western countries.[94] By not expressly naming certain practices in the West (e.g. pornography, sexist advertising or cosmetic surgery) *cultural*, the Committee runs the risk of orientalising culture.[95]

90 Using the terminology of Packer, the Committee adheres to a weak form of cultural relativism or to a pluralist perspective. See Packer 2002, p 96.

91 CO Bhutan, UN Doc.A/59/38, 31st Session (2004) para. 115.

92 CO Cambodia, CEDAW/C/KHM/CO/3 (2006) para. 17. See also CO Cook Islands, CEDAW/C/COK/CO/1 (2007) para. 22.

93 See Wohlbold 2008.

94 In that regard, one should keep in mind that, while conducting its constructive dialogue with States parties and while drafting its Concluding Observations, the Committee is to a large extend dependent upon the issues that are raised by the State party itself, or by NGOs in their shadow reports. See for a discussion of how culture, religion and tradition are brought up in country reports of especially non-Western countries Merry 2006, p 90 ff.

95 See para. 3.3.

In Committee documents we have found many concerns and recommendations about a wide variety of cultural practices that contravene Article 5 of the Convention[96], which for the sake of clarity we have summarised in five different categories.

Traditional harmful practices and beliefs

In the first place the Committee often comments on harmful customary, traditional or religious laws and practices, mostly when discussing the situation in the Arab world, in African countries and in (Central)Asian countries. Since 2007, the Committee uses a more or less standard formula about its concerns in this respect in its Concluding Observations:

> "The Committee expresses a general concern about the persistence of discriminatory stereotypes and cultural practices and traditions of a patriarchal nature relating to the roles and responsibilities of women and men in the family and in society, as they constitute serious obstacles to women's educational and professional prospects and the enjoyment of their human rights and contribute to the persistence of violence against women."[97]

A wide range of specific cultural practices and their damaging consequences for women are addressed by the Committee. It mentions inhumane rites undergone by widows, female genital mutilation and similar customs,[98] son-preference and illegal sex-selective abortion[99], traditional practices related to dowries and adultery, the practices of pre-marriage and polygamy[100], bride price or dowry[101], forced and early marriage, female genital mutilation, ritual bondage, levirate and repudiation[102], widowhood rites, food taboos[103], *Trokosi* (ritual slavery)[104], and the customary right of married men to treat their wives in the same way as minor children.[105] Also, the Committee frequently notices that cultural barriers may exist which prevent women from land ownership and participation in the

96 Often taken together with Article 2(f).

97 CO Mozambique, CEDAW/C/MOZ/CO/2 (2007) paras 20, 21. See for a list of similar references Koukoulis-Spiliotopoulos 2008, p 420, footnote 33.

98 E.g. CO Nigeria, UN Doc.A/53/38, 19th Session (1998) para. 153.

99 E.g. CO China, CEDAW/C/CHN/CO/6 (2006) para. 17.

100 CO Congo, UN Doc.A/58/38, 28th Session (2003) para. 180. CO Bhutan, UN Doc.A/59/38, 31st Session (2004) para. 115.

101 CO Botswana, CEDAW/C/BOT/CO/3 (2010) para. 23; CO Timor Leste, CEDAW/C/TLS/CO/1 (2009) para. 29. See also CO Albania, UN Doc.A/58/38, 28th Session (2003) para. 69.

102 CO Togo, CEDAW/C/TGO/CO/5 (2006) para. 14.

103 CO Guinea Bissau, CEDAW/C/GNB/CO/6 (2009) para. 23.

104 CO Ghana, CEDAW/C/GHA/CO/5 (2006) para. 21.

105 CO Botswana, CEDAW/C/BOT/CO/3 (2010) para. 23.

decision-making process.[106] It has expressed concerns about customary law that has a detrimental impact on the rights of women with regard to inheritance, matrimonial regimes and gifts,[107] and on the concept of male guardianship over women ('*mehrem*').[108]

Machismo

Secondly, the Committee is concerned about the effects of a machismo culture in the context of Caribbean and Latin American countries. The machismo attitude expected from men encourages adolescent and young males to get involved in high-risk sexual behaviour as a proof of manhood. "[…] for young men, gender stereotyping manifests in direct relation to their peers/'crews' through a strong social influence to adopt certain competitive and negative roles and sexual behavior; […]"[109] For example, it has stated that "[A]s long as stereotyped roles persisted in education and mothers encouraged their sons to adopt macho attitudes whereas girls were brought up to be docile and obedient, no change was imminent."[110] In the same document the Committee notes "(…) the prevailing attitude of machismo in the country, which affected women in all walks of life and expressed itself also in violence against women, which was largely accepted."[111] The Committee links this culture to the persistence of severe forms of violence against women in these societies: "The Committee is also concerned that the prevailing gender stereotypes and patriarchal culture and macho image of men may be contributing factors to the levels of violence against women."[112]

Protective maternity laws

Thirdly, the Committee is very concerned about the persistence of protective maternity laws that perpetuate women's primary role as mothers and childminders, especially in former communist countries in Eastern Europe and

106 E.g. CO Paraguay, UN Doc.A/51/38, 15th Session (1996) para. 126; see also CO Kyrgystan, UN Doc.A/59/38, 31st Session (2004) para. 171.

107 CO Burundi, CEDAW/C/BDI/CO/4 (2008) para. 13.

108 CO Saudi Arabia, CEDAW/C/SAU/CO/4 (2008) para. 15.

109 Common Country Assessment Report under UN Development assistance Framework for Jamaica for the period 2006–2010, p 75. www.jm.undp.org/files/CCA-_Jamaica_3-final-unct.pdf (last accessed on July 20, 2010).

110 CO Ecuador, UN Doc.A/49/38, 13th Session (1994) para. 523. See also e.g. CO Dominican Republic, UN Doc.A/53/38, 18th Session (1998) para. 334; and CO Nicaragua, UN Doc.A/56/38, 25th Session (2001) para. 294.

111 CO Ecuador, UN Doc.A/49/38, 13th Session (1994) para. 524. See also e.g. CO Cuba, UN Doc.A/55/38, 23rd Session (2000) para. 261.

112 CO Jamaica, CEDAW/C/JAM/CO/5 (2006) para. 15. See also the OP-Report on Mexico, CEDAW/C/2005/OP.8/Mexico, 27 January 2005.

Central Asia.[113] It has expressed time and again that (legal and social) over-protectiveness of women's maternal roles, very much works to the detriment of women's economic opportunities and interests: "The Committee is very concerned about the relationship between sexual stereotyping and overprotective labour legislation. It noted that protective labour laws had the sole effect of restricting women's economic opportunities, and were neither legitimate nor effective as a measure for promoting women's reproductive health. Women should have a right to free choice as to their employment (…)."[114] Or: "The Committee expresses its concern at the overemphasis on legislative protection of and cultural promotion of motherhood and family roles for women, rather than on women as individuals in their own right. The traditional, stereotyped view of women as mothers is thereby reinforced and negates the participation of fathers in childcare."[115]

Breadwinner models

In the fourth place, the Committee expresses a lot of concern about the persistence of male breadwinner models and the lack of facilities that would stimulate the sharing of responsibilities within the family in laws and policies of especially Western European and Anglo Saxon countries.[116] In its Concluding Observations the Committee has often stated that it "(…) remains concerned about the persistence of deep-rooted traditional attitudes and stereotypes regarding the roles and responsibilities of women and men in the family and in society."[117] Or it has expressed concerns about "the persistence and pervasiveness of patriarchal attitudes and deep-rooted stereotypes".[118] It is also "(…) concerned that entrenched stereotypical attitudes to women in society, and the idea of an exclusively male head of household encourages segregation in employment, and a denial of the economic contribution of women."[119]

113 See for an example from another region e.g. CO Kuwait, UN Doc.A/59/38, 31st Session (2004) para. 72.

114 CO Ukraine, UN Doc.A/51/38, 15th Session (1996) para. 286. See also e.g. CO Armenia, UN Doc.A/52/38, 17th Session (1997) para. 58; CO The Czech Republic, UN Doc.A/53/38, 18th Session (1998) para. 196; CO China, UN Doc.A/54/38, 20th Session (1999) paras 280 and 296; CO Kazakhstan, UN Doc.A/56/38, 24th Session (2001) paras 101–102.

115 CO Slovakia, UN Doc.A/53/38, 19th Session (1998) para. 74. See also CO Armenia, UN Doc.A/52/38, 17th Session (1997) para. 58.

116 See for an example from another region e.g. CO Egypt, UN Doc.A/56/38, 24th Session (2001) para. 332.

117 CO Austria, CEDAW/C/AUT/CO/6 (2007) para. 17. See also e.g. CO Greece, CEDAW/C/GRC/CO/6 (2007) para. 13; CO Germany, UN Doc.A/59/38, 31st Session (2004) para. 384; CO Cape Verde, CEDAW/C/CPV/CO/6 (2006) para. 17; CO China, CEDAW/C/CHN/CO/6 (2006) para. 17; CO Poland, CEDAW/C/POL/CO/6 (2007) para. 16.

118 CO Italy, CEDAW/C/ITA/CC/4–5 (2005) para. 25. See also CO Estonia, UN Doc.A/57/38, 26th Session (2002) paras 25, 26; CO Lithuania, UN Doc.A/55/38, 23rd Session (2000) paras 138 and 139.

119 CO Fiji Islands, UN Doc.A/57/38, 26th Session (2002) para. 31.

Gender stereotyping in education and in advertising and the media

In a great number of cases – all over the world – the Committee connects the segregation in the labour market and the limited participation of women in the public sphere in general to gender stereotypes in educational materials and to the stereotyped educational choices of girls and boys in (professional and academic) education.[120] Time and again, the Committee states that it is "(...) concerned about the consequences of gender stereotyping in curricula and the impact of the fact that girls take traditional 'female' courses and boys traditional 'male' courses on women's employment options and income,"[121] and it discusses "stereotypical cultural attitudes" which are reflected in the segregation of the labour market and in educational choices.[122] As a result of this "(...) women continue to be concentrated in a narrow range of employment."[123] In this respect, the Committee often talks about the elimination of gender stereotypes in order to facilitate "the diversification of the educational choices of boys and girls."[124]

Quite often, the Committee discusses the way in which women are depicted in their traditional family roles in advertising and in the media "The Committee "(...) is concerned that women are sometimes depicted by the media and in advertising as sex objects and in traditional roles."[125] On a few occasions the Committee notes with concern "(...) that a process of mainstreaming pornography, also known as 'sexualisation of the public sphere', is occurring in the State party."[126] Or, in a similar vein: "The Committee is concerned that media and advertising in the State party are becoming increasingly pornographic, and that the over-sexualised depiction of women strengthens the existing stereotypes of women as sex object and girls' low self-esteem."[127]

120 Many of these considerations are (also) based on Article 10(c), in which States are obliged to eliminate gender stereotyping in this area.
121 E.g. CO Trinidad and Tobago, UN Doc.A/57/38, 26th Session (2002) para. 33.
122 CO Norway, CEDAW/C/NOR/CO/7 (2007) para. 17.
123 E.g. CO France, CEDAW/C/FRA/CO/6 (2008) para. 18; CO Lebanon, CEDAW/C/LBN/CO/3 (2008) para. 24; CO Belize, CEDAW/C/BLZ/CO/4 (2007) para. 23.
124 E.g. CO Estonia, CEDAW/C/EST/CO/4 (2007) para. 13.
125 CO Germany, UN Doc.A/59/38, 31st Session (2004) para. 384; see also e.g. CO Germany, CEDAW/C/DEU/CO/6 (2009) para. 27; or CO Italy, CEDAW/C/ITA/CC/4-5 (2005) para. 25. In that context the Committee regularly uses the pejorative words 'sexist' or 'sexism'. E.g. in CO Ukraine, CEDAW/C/UKR/CO/7 (2010) para. 24.
126 CO Sweden, CEDAW/C/MAR/SWE/CO/4 (2008) para. 22. See also CO Japan, CEDAW/C/JPN/CO/6 (2009) para. 29.
127 CO Finland, CEDAW/C/FIN/ 5 and 6 (2008) para. 177.

OBLIGATIONS OF STATES PARTIES ON THE BASIS OF ARTICLE 5

The drafters of the Convention left it in the middle *how* States parties should implement their obligations under Article 5.[128] Those (few) commentators who do discuss this Article in some detail[129] also have great trouble in determining what exactly it is that States parties should do on the basis of this Article. It is seen as one of the most difficult provisions to implement. Some commentators suggest that States at the most should launch information campaigns. A thorough analysis of the way in which the CEDAW Committee deals with Article 5 in its Concluding Observation reveals that much more needs to be done. The Committee has given numerous concrete directions as to what States parties can and should do in order to achieve the aim of addressing prevailing gender relations and the persistence of gender-based stereotypes. Very briefly summarised, States parties that have signed up to the Convention have five main obligations on the basis of Article 5.[130] They have to:

- address and redress gender stereotypes that lie at the basis of direct and indirect discrimination in law and in private relations, and of violence against women in society;
- examine whether their own laws and public policies are based on gender stereotyped presumptions and if so, to remedy structural/systemic discrimination against women that follows from such stereotypes;
- address gender stereotyping in the media and in advertising, contravening at least the most degrading and overly 'sexualised' images of women;
- encourage and facilitate the sharing of parental responsibilities between men and women through legislative measures and social policies;
- launch information campaigns and educational programmes in which maternity is seen as a positive contribution to society and parents are encouraged to share responsibilities.

A GRADUAL IMPLEMENTATION OF ARTICLE 5 CEDAW

The Committee in its earlier days at some points went rather far in suggesting that a particular culture should be changed, or even abolished. Especially when it concerns practices that are somehow rooted in or connected to religion, this

---

128 Rehof 1993, p 77 ff.
129 See for an overview of the literature Holtmaat 2004, p 64 and Cook & Cusack 2010.
130 See Holtmaat 2011, for a more elaborate account of the States parties obligations under Article 5.

may be considered as inappropriate or even offensive by the State party.[131] Nowadays, it seems to be more cautious, but it is still firm about the necessity of intervention by the State party when women's human rights are violated with a call on cultural, traditional, customary or religious practices or beliefs. For example:

> "The Committee also calls on the State party to take prompt action to counteract the influence of non-State actors, which, through the misinterpretation of Islam and the use of intimidation and violence, are undermining the enjoyment by women and girls of their human rights."[132]

In order to avoid strong resistance against the modification of such religiously inspired, traditional or customary patterns of conduct, especially from the side of fundamentalist religious or traditionalist leaders, a cautious, gradual implementation of Article 5 CEDAW is required. The Committee has recognised this, where it stated that

> "[W]hile respecting the stages in Morocco's political, economic, sociological and cultural evolution and the need for the population to support any reform concerning women's rights, the Committee encouraged the Government to persevere in using 'ijtihad', which was the evolving interpretation of religious texts so as to give the necessary impetus to the improvement of the status of women and thus gradually to change attitudes."[133]

However, this does not mean that States parties may shield behind their culture as an excuse to stay inactive in this field. In 2002, the Committee decided that its Concluding Observations would include a section on "factors and difficulties" affecting the implementation of the Convention and concluded that the "persistence of stereotypical attitudes relating to the roles of women and men" would not be categorised as such a "factor or difficulty."[134] In line with this, the Committee has stated that it "is particularly concerned about the State party's limited efforts to address directly such discriminatory practices and stereotypes and its position that the current widespread support for and adherence to these practices would prevent compliance with legislative measures designed to eliminate them."[135]

---

131 The 1974 report of the constructive dialogue with the Libyan Arab Jamahiriya, for example shows little respect for the freedom of religion: "Members felt that the interpretation of the Koran had to be reviewed in the light of the provisions of the Convention and in the light of the current social environment." CO Libyan Arab Jamahiriya, UN Doc.A/49/38, 13th Session (1994) para. 130.

132 CO Pakistan, CEDAW/C/PAK/CO/3 (2007) para. 29.

133 CO Morocco, UN Doc.A/52/38, 16th Session (1997) para. 71.

134 See A/57/38, 27th Session (2002) para. 374.

135 CO Gabon, CEDAW/C/GAB/CC 2-5 (2005) para. 30.

OTHER INTERNATIONAL DOCUMENTS EXPRESSING THE SAME CONCERNS AS ARTICLE 5 CEDAW

In line with Article 5 CEDAW and the comments of the CEDAW Committee, many international documents contain provisions or considerations about the necessity to change all those cultural customs, practices and beliefs that are detrimental to the full enjoyment of women's human rights. A most clear example is a General Comment made by the UN Committee on Economic, Social and Cultural Rights:

> "Gender-based assumptions and expectations generally place women at a disadvantage with respect to substantive enjoyment of rights, such as freedom to act and to be recognized as autonomous, fully capable adults, to participate fully in economic, social and political development, and to make decisions concerning their circumstances and conditions. Gender-based assumptions about economic, social and cultural roles preclude the sharing of responsibility between men and women in all spheres that is necessary to equality."[136]

The General Comment on Article 3 of the ICCPR, adopted by the UN Human Rights Committee, clarifies that:

> "[I]nequality in the enjoyment of rights by women throughout the world is deeply embedded in tradition, history and culture, including religious attitudes. The subordinate role of women in some countries is illustrated by the high incidence of prenatal sex selection and abortion of female foetuses. States parties should ensure that traditional, historical, religious or cultural attitudes are not used to justify violations of women's right to equality before the law and to equal enjoyment of all Covenant rights."[137]

There are many other examples of provisions in international human rights law that declare the same principles and concerns as are expressed in Article 5 CEDAW.[138]

---

[136] CESCR General Comment 16, E/C.12/2005/4, 13 May 2005, para. 14. See also CESCR General Comment 20, E/C.12/GC/20, 25 May 2009, para. 20.

[137] UNHRC General Comment no 28, The equality of rights between men and women, UN Doc. HRC, CCPR/C/221/Rev.1/Add.10, 29 March 2000, para. 5.

[138] See e.g. the *Inter-American Convention on the Prevention, Punishment and Eradication of Violence against Women* (Convention of Belém do Pará 1994): Articles 7(e) and 8(b). Or see the *Protocol to the African Charter on Human and Peoples' Rights on the Rights of Women in Africa* (2003): Articles 2(2), 4(d), 6 and 13.

WOMEN'S HUMAN RIGHTS TAKING PRIORITY OVER CULTURE

In many of its Concluding Observations the CEDAW Committee has expressly stated that violations of women's human rights can not be excused with an appeal to culture, tradition or religion. For example, it has made it clear that "(...) cultural characteristics could not be allowed to undermine the principle of the universality of human rights, which remained inalienable and non-negotiable, nor to prevent the adoption of appropriate measures in favour of women."[139] Or that "(...) cultural and religious values cannot be allowed to undermine the universality of women's rights."[140] Women's human rights should have primacy "over contradictory norms of customary law."[141] Or, in yet another case: "The Committee is concerned by the State party's constant citing of religious principles and cultural specificities to justify why the status of women has not kept up with the overall advances of society."[142] Sometimes this concern is connected to the growth of religious fundamentalism in a particular country. For example, the Committee has remarked that it

> "(...) is concerned that, although Azerbaijan is a secular State in which the provisions of the Convention should be relatively easy to implement, there is, as yet, insufficient governmental commitment to eliminating deeply rooted patriarchal attitudes and avoiding the danger of the insurgence of fundamentalist tendencies, which impedes the full implementation of the Convention, in particular the measures outlined in subparagraph (a) of article 5."[143] And the Committee has noticed "(...) the rise of religious fundamentalist groups advocating restrictive interpretations of sharia law, which discriminate against women, in several regions of the country."[144]

In other (especially African) countries, not religious fundamentalism, but traditionalism under the guise of preserving national identity is at stake: "The Committee also expresses concern about information received regarding the promotion, by some sectors of Mozambican society, of conservative views contesting women's human rights on the basis of cultural values and the preservation of national identity."[145] In a similar vein the Committee has a problem with a recourse to so-called Asian values[146]:

---

139 CO Morocco, UN Doc.A/52/38, 16th Session (1997) para. 64.

140 CO Indonesia, UN Doc.A/53/38, 18th Session (1998) para. 282.

141 CO Vanuatu, CEDAW/C/VUT/CO/3 (2007) para. 10.

142 CO Algeria, Un Doc. A/54/38, 20th Session (1999) para. 71.

143 CO Azerbaijan, UN Doc.A/53/38, 18th Session (1998) para. 58. See also CO Turkey, UN Doc.A/52/38, 16th Session (1997) para. 164.

144 CO Indonesia, CEDAW/C/EST/IDN/CO/5 (2007) para. 12.

145 CO Mozambique, CEDAW/C/MOZ/CO/2 (2007) para. 22.

146 The Committee here refers to the so-called Bangkok Declaration, adopted on 7 April 1993 by the Asian regional meeting preceding the Vienna World Conference on Human Rights; see UN Doc. A/Conf.157/ASRM/8-A/CONF.157/PC/59 (1993):3.

> "While the Committee recognises the importance of the family as the basic social unit, it expresses concern that the concept of Asian values regarding the family, including that of the husband having the legal status of head of household, might be interpreted so as to perpetuate stereotyped gender roles in the family and reinforce discrimination against women."[147]

From all this, it follows that in the eyes of the CEDAW Committee the principles of women's equality and non-discrimination clearly prevail over claims about the (positive) values of religion, culture or tradition and the need or wish of States parties to preserve these values in a rapidly modernising and integrating or assimilating world.

2.5 THE RIGHT TO CULTURE AND ITS LIMITS

In legal discussions about the topic of women's human rights and culture, this issue is often phrased as a clash or as a fundamental incompatibility of two different rights that in principle have equal standing as a *human* right.[148] The prioritisation of women's human rights over culture, made by the CEDAW Committee, therefore is contested. Opponents claim that the right to culture has at least an equal standing. Therefore no solution to the clash is said to exist, or in any individual case a 'weighing of interests' needs to take place between women's human rights and the right to culture. This is even more so the case when the specific culture at hand is a religion.[149] The importance of women's human rights, in such a reasoning, becomes 'relative', meaning that it becomes subject to an evaluation in which other rights are seen as at least equally important. For the purpose of engaging into a fruitful dialogue about women's human rights and culture, this line of reasoning is particularly hazardous since it easily leads the participants of this dialogue into a loophole of contesting or conflicting rights, from which no escape seems to be possible.[150] In this paragraph we therefore discuss the concept of the 'human right to culture', as well as the limits that are posed in several international documents to the exercising of any such right.

---

147 CO Singapore, UN Doc.A/56/38, 25th Session (2001) para. 79.

148 See for a description of this clash para. 1.2. In the following, we include religion within the wider concept of culture. The rights to freedom of religion and non – discrimination on that ground may even seem to be a stronger right than the right to enjoy one's culture. We will return to this issue in para. 3.4.

149 See also para. 3.4.

150 It presupposes that the essence or absolute content of each of these rights may be established in an objective and independent way (by lawyers or by judges). Thereby it denies the fact that legal rights are also a site for political/social struggle over their meaning in a particular context and time. See Baer 2010, p 64.

THE RIGHT TO CULTURE: DOES IT EXIST AND WHERE?

In the legal literature about human rights, several categories of human rights are being distinguished, according to the titles of the two main UN human rights Covenants, i.e. the *International Covenant on Civil and Political Rights* (ICCPR) and the *International Covenant on Economic, Social and Cultural Rights* (ICESCR). Although the term 'culture' appears in the title of the latter Covenant, the concept of cultural rights is far less developed than the concepts of political, civil, economic and social rights.[151] This may be due to the fact that there exists no definite or firm legal definition of what 'culture' may entail. Culture may be interpreted narrowly in terms of artistic expressions, literature, music, dance, et cetera. But it may also indicate 'a whole way of life', which includes almost everything that human beings have constructed among themselves.[152]

A much quoted definition of culture is the one used in the 2001 UNESCO *Universal Declaration on Cultural Diversity*, in which culture includes "(...) the set of distinctive spiritual, material, intellectual and emotional features of society or of a social group, (...) [which] encompasses, in addition to art and literature, lifestyles, ways of living together, value systems, traditions and beliefs."[153] Culture is a "broad, inclusive concept encompassing all manifestations of human existence. (...) Culture shapes and mirrors the values of well-being, as well as the economic, social and political life of individuals, groups of individuals and communities."[154] In these (and other) documents, culture is seen as something positive which gives meaning and structure to individual human lives and which enables human beings to develop their full human capacities and capabilities. Culture, thus seen, is an important tool for empowerment. As such it deserves the full and effective protection of international human rights instruments.

If culture is defined in such a wide way, many different rights that are relevant for sustaining or protecting a particular culture may be found in various international and regional human rights documents. The aspect of religion, for instance, is protected in the ICCPR (Article 18), while other aspects, like the right to participate in cultural life or to enjoy one's culture are regulated in the ICSECR (Article 15(1) sub a) and in the ICCPR (Article 27). In CEDAW Article 13(c) requires States to take all appropriate measures to eliminate discrimination against women "in all aspects of cultural life". In fact, one may hold that most human rights – even when the term 'culture' is not mentioned

151 Recently, the concept gets a little more attention in legal literature. See e.g. Donders 2009, Donders 2002 and Francioni & Scheinin (eds) 2008.

152 Donders 2009, p 814.

153 Preamble of the Declaration, as cited by Donders 2009.

154 UN CESCR General Comment 21, 20 November 2009, UN DOC E/C. 12/GC/21, paras 11 and 13.

explicitly – do have important cultural aspects. The right to freedom of association, for example, only gets a meaning when people associate themselves on the basis of what brings them together, which is part of their 'way of life'. And the content to the right to food is co-determined by cultural practices and beliefs surrounding the production and consumption of food. Various lists of so-called cultural rights appear in the literature. Such a list is not presented here, since we agree that indeed most human rights (be it civil, political, social, economic or cultural) do have cultural aspects that hardly may be separated from these rights. Three international documents, adopted by UNESCO, are of particular importance for the recognition of the importance of cultural rights. These are the *Declaration of Principles of International Cultural Co-operation* (1966), the *Universal Declaration on Cultural Diversity* (2001), and the *Convention on the Protection and Promotion of Cultural Expressions* (2005).[155] With the inclusion of such cultural rights in general human rights documents and the adoption of these specific Declarations and Conventions it is acknowledged that cultural rights do protect crucial aspects of human life and human dignity, and that systemic and structural violations of such rights may lead to serious ethnic, religious and / or cultural conflicts within a State.[156]

THE RIGHT TO CULTURE: INDIVIDUAL OR COLLECTIVE?

A particular problematic aspect of the concept of the human right to culture is that it is not always clear to whom such a right belongs, i.e. who may claim that a particular culture or cultural expression or practice should not be violated, or to put it positively: that it should be sustained or protected, be accommodated or supported? Is it individuals who are members of a particular culture, or is it the cultural group as such?

With the exclusion of Articles 1 of the ICCPR and ICSECR, which guarantee the right to national sovereignty to States, human rights belong to individual human beings. That means that each and every individual has been guaranteed by international documents that these rights will not be violated. If violation nevertheless takes place, the individual may stand up (if necessary in court) against such 'malpractice'.[157] As for cultural rights, however, frequently the claim is made that these rights belong to the cultural group as such. Or, in the words of Susanne Baer, claims of a right to culture often amount to 'groupism'. Such a claim is very problematic, in her view: "Whenever a 'culture' or a 'religion' claims

155 Described by Donders 2009, p 825 ff.

156 Donders 2009, p 814.

157 Some legal systems allow for public interest groups to act on behalf of individual victims of (human) rights violations or to take public – group – action. However, the starting point remains that individual rights are at stake, not rights of the group as such.

recognition, we have the problem of reification, in that this suggests that the culture or religion is homogenous. We also usually have the problem of elitism, since and when such collective claims are not defined by all members of the relevant entity. In addition, (...), we have the problem of mapping the world in exclusionary blocs."[158] Therefore, we have to clearly distinguish between the right to freely enjoy /practice a culture by individual members within it – without any form of discrimination between them – and the right of a cultural group: "To be sure, an individual right is a right of individuals in communities, but not a right of the community which can be turned against the individual."[159] Any claim of a right of a cultural group or community raises the difficult question as to who in that case may claim such a right on behalf of the group, and what happens if members of the group have a different understanding or interpretation of the culture at stake. In that regard it should be remembered that part of the human rights of all people, is the right to interpret and to develop the culture (and religion), as was clearly expressed by the Human Rights Committee, in its General Comment on *Equality of Rights between Men and Women*:

> "States parties must ensure that freedom of thought, conscience and religion, and the freedom to adopt the religion or belief of one's choice – including the freedom to change religion and belief and to express one's religion and belief – will be guaranteed and protected in law and in practice for both men and women, on the same terms and without discrimination."[160]

Also, it should be stressed that the CEDAW Convention itself provides in Article 13(c) that women have the right to non-discrimination in respect to *all aspects of cultural life*. This means that women have the right – on a basis of equality with men – to participate in describing and developing cultural norms and practices and, in interpreting them, et cetera.

In 2009, after long and fierce discussions, the UN Human Rights Council decided to install an Independent Expert in the Field of Cultural Rights, with a mandate for three years.[161] Some of the difficult issues that this Expert needs to address are which rights may be labelled as such and to what extent these rights may be perceived as group rights. In the latter case, it is crucial how it is guaranteed that all group members have a right to participate in defining the content and rules of the particular culture. In the document in which the mandate of this Expert was described, it has been stressed that cultural rights are an integral part of human

---

158 Baer 2010, p 59. In this quote she refers to R. Brubacker, *Ethnicity without Groups*, 2006. Baer warns against legal recognition of group rights, since "a collective freedom tends to trump individual rights." (Ibid, p 60).

159 Baer 2010, p 60/61.

160 General Comment 28, UN HRC, CCPR/C/221/Rev.1/Add.10, para. 21.

161 UN Doc A/HRC/10/L23, 26 March 2009. Farida Shaheed, from Pakistan, was appointed as the first Independent Expert in this field.

rights, and that respect for cultural diversity is a leading principle, while at the same time repeating the idea of the universality of human rights. The document thereby recognises that respect for cultural diversity and recognising cultural rights may possibly undermine the idea of universality of human rights. In past decades in many international documents it has been stressed that this is not allowed. Most importantly, this is expressed in the Vienna Declaration (1993):

> "While the significance of national and regional particularities and various historical, cultural and religious backgrounds must be borne in mind, it is the duty of States, regardless of their political, economic and cultural systems, to promote and protect all human rights and fundamental freedoms."[162]

Furthermore, the Vienna Declaration stresses the importance of "the eradication of any conflicts which may arise between the rights of women and the harmful effects of certain traditional or customary practices, cultural prejudices and religious extremism."[163]

THE LIMITS TO EXERCISING THE RIGHT TO CULTURE

The CEDAW Committee does not stand alone in its opinion that a call upon culture, tradition, religion, customs, or even upon the right to culture as such, may not lead to the acceptance of violations of women's human rights, as guaranteed under this Convention. The same idea is expressed in the Vienna Declaration, quoted above: respect for cultural diversity or cultural rights may not lead to undermining the universality of human rights, in the sense that these rights belong to *all* persons, irrespective of the question to which cultural community they belong.[164] A general restriction clause exists in Article 29(3) of the Universal Declaration of Human Rights, which stipulates that these rights and freedoms may in no case be exercised contrary to the purposes and principles of the United Nations. One of these principles is the principle of equality and non-discrimination. The principle that women's human rights may not be put aside under the guise of respect for cultural rights, is also clearly expressed in

---

162 Vienna Declaration and Programme of Action of 12 July 1993, UN Doc. A/CONF.157/23, para. 5. See also the UNESCO Declaration on Cultural Diversity, Paris 2001, Preamble and Article 5.

163 Vienna Declaration, para. 38. The 1995 Beijing Declaration expresses similar viewpoints, but adds that "full respect for various religious and ethical values (...) should contribute to the full enjoyment by women of their human rights." *Report of the Fourth World Conference on Women*, UN Doc. A/CONF.177/20, para. 9. See Otto 1997, p 12.

164 This is one meaning of the concept of universality of human rights; another is that the content of such rights is the same / should be interpreted and implemented in the same manner everywhere on the earth. See about this issue also para. 4.1 (under the heading 'universality or cultural relativity?').

various restriction clauses which are attached to specific provisions that guarantee certain aspects of the right to culture.[165]

In these provisions, on the one hand it is acknowledged that there is indeed a right to live according to one's cultural traditions or beliefs and a right to practise one's culture or religious beliefs. On the other hand, however, it is provided that these rights only exist under the condition that the human rights of others/ women are not restricted or violated. So, for example all international documents that guarantee the freedom of expression (including cultural expressions!), have bound this freedom to the restriction that the exercise of this right does not lead to the violation of the rights of others. This includes the rights of others not to be discriminated against, e.g. on the ground of sex or gender. Both the *European Convention on Human Rights* (ECHR, Article 9) and *the International Convention on Civil and Political Rights* (ICCPR, Article 18) allow restrictions of the right to manifest one's religion in order to protect the rights and freedoms of others. Women's right not to be discriminated falls within the scope of that limitation. According to the Human Rights Committee, "Article 18 may not be relied upon to justify discrimination against women by reference to freedom of thought, conscience and religion."[166] Although Article 27 ICCPR (guaranteeing minority's rights to enjoy their culture) does not include a similar exception clause, the Human Rights Committee has expressly stated that the rights that are guaranteed under this Article do not authorise any State, group or person to violate women's human rights under the Covenant.[167]

Another example of prioritising women's human rights over culture can be found in the UNESCO *Convention on the Protection and Promotion of Cultural Expressions* (2005), stating in Article 2 as a first Guiding Principle that there should be respect for human rights and fundamental freedoms:

> "Cultural diversity can be protected and promoted only if human rights and fundamental freedoms, such as freedom of expression, information and communication, as well as the ability of individuals to choose cultural expressions, are guaranteed. No one may invoke the provisions of this Convention in order to infringe human rights and fundamental freedoms as enshrined in the Universal Declaration of Human Rights or guaranteed by international law, or to limit the scope thereof."

This same principle is reflected in many other documents. For example, the *Declaration on the Elimination of Violence Against Women* (DEVAW), prohibits

---

165 See also Koukoulis-Spiliotopoulos 2008 and Raday 2003, 2007 and 2008.
166 UN HRC, General Comment 28, 'The equality of rights between men and women', 29 March 2000, UN Doc. CCPR/C/21/Rev.1/Add.10, para. 21.
167 See Ibid, para. 32. See also Raday 2008, p 601.

States to invoke custom, tradition, or religious considerations in order to avoid their obligations, *inter alia* to protect women from violence committed by private parties.[168] In the same vein, the official mandate for the Independent Expert in the Field of Cultural Rights includes the explicit provision that no-one may invoke the right to cultural diversity while thereby violating the human rights of others.[169]

Of particular importance for the topic of the relationship between women's human rights and religion is the study that was conducted in 2002 by the UN Special Rapporteur on Freedom of Religion or Belief, Abdelfattah Amor.[170] The Rapporteur explicitly refers to Article 5 (and 2) CEDAW and concludes that it is not the objective of the Convention to intervene in religions, but solely to encourage States to modify those traditions that are *damaging* or *negative* for women. The Rapporteur takes the stance that discrimination of women can not be justified on the ground of religion, where he argues that "[c]ulture, religion, and freedom of religion or belief are relative notions, while respect for life, human dignity, non-discrimination and women's rights are invariants which can serve to unite humanity."[171] In a 2009 report of Asma Jahangir, the (then) Rapporteur, it was acknowledged that religious practices and activities might impose severe restrictions on women.[172]

Many international organs warn against the unconditional reference to the right to culture, or against the suggestion that religion or tradition may represent absolute normative values which may (always and automatically) overrule human rights norms. This warning comes as a reaction to States who publicly argue in International Organisations that religion and tradition should be valued higher and should play an important role in the development and interpretation or implementation of human rights. Exemplary for this development is the Resolution about the positive contribution of traditional values proposed by Russia, and adopted with a 26–15 (and 6 abstentions) vote in a meeting of the UN Human Rights Council in 2009.[173]

---

168 UN Doc /RES/48/104, 20 December 1993, Article 4.

169 UN Doc A/HRC/10/L23, para. 4.

170 Report of the UN Special Rapporteur on Freedom of Religion or Belief, 5 April 2002, UN Doc. E/CN.4/2002/73/Add.2.

171 Ibid, para. 58.

172 Report of the UN Special Rapporteur on Freedom of Religion or Belief, 21 December 2009, UN Doc. A/HRC/13/40, in particular paras 37, 45, 46 and 58.

173 HRC 12th session 2009; See www.wluml.org/fr/node/5581 (last accessed on July 20, 2010).

CHAPTER 3
CULTURE AND GENDER

"Although culture is a term on everyone's lips, people rarely talk about what they mean by it."[1]

"Attempts to make normative judgements and to change behaviour, must be premised on the understanding that cultures, including our own, are patriarchal – not more or less so, but differently patriarchal."[2]

This Chapter is dedicated to the aspect of culture in our question about how we can move from a deadlock to a dialogue about women's human rights and culture. Culture is closely linked to the construction of identity, both on the level of social or ethnic groups or of nations or nationalities, and on the level of the family and individual men and women. In that way, there is a firm relationship between culture and gender. The latter term refers to the way in which the physical or biological categories of the male and female sex get – an often static and fixed – meaning and structure through the intermediate of culture. In the previous Chapter, it was explained that Article 5 CEDAW contains the obligation to modify gender stereotypes and fixed parental gender roles. In this Chapter we explain in some detail what these concepts entail. This Chapter further discusses how it is possible that culture sometimes may contribute positively to the improvement of women's human rights, but unfortunately in many instances functions as an important obstacle in achieving this objective. What causes interpretations and applications of cultures in such a way that they are at odds with the human rights of women? Our analysis reveals that a most important obstacle to changing persistently unequal and oppressive gender relations is not culture as such, but the widely held belief of cultural essentialism. By whom and why is this belief voiced in the debates about women's human rights? Finally, we discuss whether religion takes a special place among the wide diversity of cultural expressions and values.

---

1 Merry 2006, p 10.
2 Volpp 2001, p 1217.

3.1 CULTURE AND IDENTITY

SOCIAL AND IDEOLOGICAL CULTURE

In paragraph 2.5 we have discussed that it is difficult to give a clear (legal) definition of culture. Culture entails such phenomena as language, shared beliefs or ideals, traditional music, national hymns, historical events and heroes, images and art, sports, local customs and traditions, laws, societal organisations and institutions and religion and religious institutions. The term culture commonly refers to *the set of shared characteristics of a particular community or nation*: they are spiritual, material, intellectual and emotional features of human experience, created in human interaction both on the level of private and public relations; culture includes religion, custom and tradition as stable or stabilising factors,[3] but at the same time is constantly produced and reproduced in a dynamic and progressive way. In fact these are all *social constructs* that are foundational to human society, though not on the same level.[4] "Culture is a macro-concept, definitive of human society, and the concept of cultural practices thus subsumes the religious norms of societies. Custom is the way in which the traditionalist cultural norms are sustained in a society."[5] Other important mechanisms to make sure that a culture is not extinguished under the influence of (sometimes profound and radical) changes in the conditions of life, including technical revolutions and globalisation[6], are social and economic arrangements, political structures, and legal regulations.[7] These legal norms, structures and institutions at the same time *reflect* and *reproduce / sustain* a particular culture.

Culture thus entails both *objective factors* (for example language, buildings, art, institutions (e.g. the family), sports, et cetera) and *subjective or ideological factors* (e.g. beliefs, political ideologies, religion, normative structures, et cetera). In practice such objective and subjective factors can hardly be separated from each other. This may be demonstrated by the example of the family, which is both an institution that is demarcated by legal rules (e.g. about who can marry and who are defined as family members), and a comprehensive system of ideas, morals and social rules about what constitutes a 'proper' family.

---

3 Raday 2003, p 665.

4 NB: in the final paragraph of this Chapter we discuss that this secular stance is highly contested by those who believe that especially religion is not man made.

5 Raday 2008, p 599.

6 This of crucial importance in a time of globalisation of cultural expressions. E.g. McDonalds and Coca Cola taking over from traditional food and drink production.

7 Merry 2006, p 15. Traditional French cheese, German beer or Italian olive oil are protected under European Union legislation against the absolute working of the principle of the free market!

Two manifestations of culture are particularly relevant for our topic: *social culture*, which pertains to people's forms of social organisation – i.e. how people interact and organise themselves in groups, and *ideological culture* – i.e. what people think, value, believe and hold as ideals. Culture is thus closely connected with the diverse ways in which social groups construct their lives ideologically, economically, socially, legally and politically. It determines to a high degree what certain experiences and practices mean for people.[8] It is often seen as the *basis* of national, ethnic or religious identities. Within a particular country, different cultures and identities may coexist at the same time. Cultural perceptions and norms are produced at different levels of society. They may be shaped along the lines of ethnic or religious differences and they may be informed by various institutions, such as the family, workplace, church and state. Hence, there may be dominant cultures and minority subcultures, or a mosaic of subcultures. Additionally, global cultural traits are increasingly traversing national boundaries, including an international human rights culture.[9]

CULTURE AND SOCIAL CHANGE

Culture is thus lived by people in a continuous process of interaction and is constantly being produced and reproduced. It therefore seems obvious to conclude that cultures vary according to context as they do over time. This is also the view that is held in current (cultural) anthropological literature.[10] In the words of a General Comment of the ESCR Committee: "The expression 'cultural life' is an explicit reference to culture as a living process, historical, dynamic and evolving, with a past, a present and a future."[11] The best indication of living and fluid cultural norms can be found in an analysis of the everyday interactions between people in a particular context. Assertions about the 'definite nature' of a certain culture will often fail to capture the entire social reality. In fact, the incongruity between social reality and ideological systems (laws, procedures, customs, rituals, beliefs and symbols) is a feature of social life in any society. Customs, laws, rituals and rigid procedures precisely serve as cultural frameworks that attempt to capture cultural and social change.

Any cultural framework risks being appreciated as an objective and neutral 'fact' that is static, homogenous and detached from power as well as from the

8 For example: when Dutch people are asked what 'Sinterklaas' means for them, many of them will give a range of answers that refer to some 'Dutch tradition' that symbolises and creates space for 'typical Dutch *gezelligheid*" (cosiness).

9 Raday 2003, p 666. See also Merry 2003 and Merry 2006.

10 See Merry 2003 Polar, who discusses the developments in anthropological theory in this regard. See also Merry 2006; Narayan 1998, Mehra, 2007 and Nyamu 2000.

11 UN CESCR General Comment 21, 20 November 2009, UN DOC E/C. 12/GC/21, para. 11.

particular economic and social circumstances in which it operates. People take the framework as it stands at a certain moment as 'true' and 'everlasting', often without realising its change over time.[12] Moreover, general statements often present cultural norms in a rigid manner and overlook variations and the conflicts inherent within actual practice.[13] Such statements are not neutral descriptions of a community's way of life. In fact, culture is not monolithic and unambiguous, having only one fixed and determined meaning. It notably embraces both the *commonly held meanings* that allow for the continuation of everyday practice as well as the *competing meanings* that galvanise change over time.[14] In other words: any culture entails aspects that make it sustainable and aspects that make it eligible for change. Cultures that are not able to adapt themselves to changing conditions of life are not viable.

CULTURE AND THE CONSTRUCTION OF IDENTITY

Culture plays an important role in the construction of identity, be it on the level of a *social group* or *nation* or on the level of the *individual human being* and their intimate *family relations*.[15] Many philosophers and cultural anthropologists "(…) have proposed that the construction of one's own identity (…) is indeed a project for every human life", and at the same time they hold it that "collective identities are a resource for that self-creation and not just a hindrance".[16] Culture thus is an important (re)source for collective and individual identities. Individual identity concerns people's personal perception / belief of who they are, what they are, and the way they see themselves in relation to 'others' – including other human beings, nature, metaphysical entities or human existence as such. Without culture no such identity formation can take place.

The question then becomes whether elements of a particular culture "contribute to an identity of its individual members in which they learn to see themselves as *dignified* and *equal* 'actors' who may take an important role in the course of their own lives? To the extent that existing norms, enforced through public action, construct an identity as lacking in dignity, or have built into them the

12 Below (in para. 3.3) we discuss how this aspect of continuous change is being denied in 'cultural essentialism'.

13 Falk Moore 1978, Ch.1.

14 UN Special Rapporteur on VAW, 'Intersections between culture and violence against women'; 17 January 2007, UN Doc. A/HRC/4/34, para. 8.

15 Appiah 2000, p 52, and Appiah 1994.

16 Appiah 2000, p 51. NB, it should be noted that this understanding of the role of culture in identity formation links up with the enlightenment value orientation, as described in para. 2.1., in which rationality and individual autonomy are deemed crucial features of all human beings.

inferiorisation of those who bear it, they are not such instruments."[17] Any culture that leads to a negative, unequal and undignified personal identity of some of its members, in terms of being inferior to other members or subjugated to their absolute power, contravenes the basic underlying values of human rights for all.[18]

3.2 CULTURE AND GENDER

NATURAL OR SOCIALLY CONSTRUCTED DIFFERENCES BETWEEN THE SEXES?

A most important feature of any culture are ideas and constructs that relate to gender, i.e. the way a culture perceives the different characteristics of the two biological / physical male and female sexes. There seems to be a sharp division between those who believe that male and female human beings are inherently different because of their essential different biology or physical fabric, and others who maintain that most or all differences between the sexes are invented and constructed by human beings and therefore are cultural.

If little girls like to play with dolls, while little boys play with toy cars or do computer games, is this reflecting 'nature' or 'nurture'? Adherents to the nature side of the debate often ascribe a whole range of essential and inherent biological or physical differences to the two sexes, generally on the basis of statistical averages, exemplifying that males and females perform differently in psychological, sociological or physiological empirical research. No matter how scientifically proven some of these differences may be, research also shows that "(…) people dramatically overestimate the magnitude of emotional differences between men and women, just as they overestimate the magnitude of other sex differences, such as differences in math and language ability."[19] More often than not, such differences are generated through implicit bias or prejudice, of which people are not at all aware. With respect to having the capacity for mathematics, of which 70% of respondents in an *Implicit Association Test* said that this 'belongs to boys' (while language ability 'belongs to girls'), it is proven that young children of both sexes have the same natural capacitates to do math.[20] However, under the influence of prejudice and stereotypes, the actual performances of boys and

---

17 Ibid.

18 See para. 2.1.

19 Hernández-Truyol 2002, p 113, footnote 10, quoting from an address by Martin Heesacker at the University of Florida Levin College of Law, Oct. 5, 2001.

20 In many countries, young boys and girls have the same scores in the so-called TIMMS-test. See e.g. Nosak et al., *Proceedings of the National Academy of Science*, 30 June 2009.

girls later in their school career will indeed differ, according to how strong in their country the implicit prejudice or bias is.[21]

The concept of 'gender' was first introduced by women's studies and gender studies in the 1980s and 1990s[22] in order to distinguish between biological or physical differences (notably with respect to childbearing and breastfeeding capacities of women) and socially constructed differences (often closely linked to these different reproductive capacities). This terminology was first used in the public international relations arena during the 1995 UN Women's Conference in Beijing, and has since become the *lingua franca* of most advocates of women's human rights.[23] In past decades, within international agencies and in meetings where women's human rights were on the political and legal agenda, a certain degree of agreement has been reached about the fact that actual differences between men and women and the way they function in life to a high degree are cultural perceptions and constructions.

The concept of gender refers to:

> "(...) the social meanings given to biological sex differences. It is an ideological and cultural construct, but is also reproduced within the realm of material practices; in turn it influences the outcomes of such practices. It affects the distribution of resources, wealth, work, decision-making and political power, and enjoyment of rights and entitlements within the family as well as public life. Despite variations across cultures and over time, gender relations throughout the world entail asymmetry of power between men and women as a pervasive trait. Thus, gender is a social stratifier, and in this sense it is similar to other stratifiers such as race, class, ethnicity, sexuality, and age. It helps us understand the social construction of gender identities and the unequal structure of power that underlies the relationship between the sexes."[24]

Consequently, in international human rights discourse, the concept of (prohibition of) sex discrimination has gradually evolved to (also) include discrimination on the ground of gender. As was expressed by the UN Committee on Economic, Social and Cultural Rights, in its General Comment on the principle of non-discrimination in the ICESCR: "Since the adoption of the Covenant, the notion of the prohibited ground 'sex' has evolved considerably to

---

21 The *Implicit Association Test* can be found at http://implicit.harvard.edu (last accessed on July 20, 2010).

22 Some important contributions are e.g. Wallach Scott 1989 and Gherardi 1994.

23 Nowadays, people often use the words sex and gender interchangeably. However, sometimes it might be useful to keep distinguishing between these terms. See para. 4.3, where we discuss that the claim for (formal) sex equality in some contexts is already revolutionary enough.

24 *1999 World Survey on the Role of Women in Development*, United Nations, New York, 1999, page ix, as cited in footnote 2 in CEDAW GR 25.

cover not only *physiological* characteristics but also the social construction of *gender* stereotypes, prejudices and expected roles, which have created obstacles to the equal fulfilment of economic, social and cultural rights."[25] The Committee links this gender discrimination to the concept of systemic or structural discrimination, where it states that it has regularly observed that "discrimination against some groups is pervasive and persistent and deeply entrenched in social behaviour and organisation" and is laid down in "legal rules, policies, practices or predominant cultural attitudes."[26]

GENDER STEREOTYPES AND FIXED PARENTAL GENDER ROLES

Crucial in the understanding of the relationship between gender and culture is the functioning of gender stereotypes and fixed parental gender roles.[27] The term 'gender stereotypes' refers to the fact that in cultural practices, language, beliefs and images as well as in (social and legal) constructs and institutions, the two distinct categories 'male' and 'female' are pictured and presented as truthful accounts of what it ultimately means to be a man *or* to be a woman. A stereotype can be defined as "(…) a generalized view or preconception of attributes or characteristics possessed by, or the roles that are or should be performed by, members of a particular group (e.g., women, lesbians, adolescents)."[28] Stereotypes tend to fixate gender identities and gender roles and make them appear as real, universal, eternal, natural, essential and/or unchangeable. They define our expectations about appropriate behaviour of and locations for men and women in society.[29] The construction of gender stereotypes ultimately rests upon the assumption that there are two *opposite* and *mutually exclusive* sexes.[30] In that way, gender stereotypes contribute to the construction of 'separate spheres' between women's world – located in private life – and men's world – located in public life.[31]

Gender stereotypes can be about physical difference between the sexes, about (assumed or real) psychological characteristics of men or women, about different male and female sexuality, or about different sex roles, or they can be

25 UN CESCR, General Comment 20, UN Doc. A/C/12/GC/20, 25 May 2009, para. 20.
26 Ibid, para. 12.
27 Gender stereotypes and fixed parental gender roles are also addressed in Article 5 CEDAW; see paras 2.3 and 2.4. We first deal with stereotypes, then turn to fixed parental gender roles.
28 Cook & Cusack 2010, p 9.
29 Moller Okin 1989, p 9; Hernández-Truyol 2002, p 111.
30 This means that transsexual or intersexual people *by definition* do not fit into the picture. See Butler 1990, p 1–34 and 110–128.
31 The public-private divide is the most persistent expression of women's and men's separate roles and identities. See e.g. Pateman 1988 and Amaya-Castro 2010.

compounded of several of these factors.[32] They come in two main forms: descriptive and prescriptive or normative.[33]

DESCRIPTIVE AND PRESCRIPTIVE GENDER STEREOTYPES

Above, it was explained that people who attach great weight to the natural differences between men and women, often construct such differences on the basis of generalisations from statistical deviations between male and female characteristics and behavioural patters, which are established in empirical research. Such generalisations are called 'evidence based' or 'factual' descriptive gender stereotypes.[34] Males are said to have more capacity to do math, think more rational, have more physical strength, or be more competitive or aggressive, while females are said to have a set of opposite characteristics. Although figures from empirical research reflect *averages*, i.e.: although there are for instance some women who do have more physical strength as compared to the average male person, *all* men and women are treated differently on the basis of these unequal statistical divides. That is: *all* women are treated as having not enough physical strength to do a particular heavy job. When an employer advertises for such a job, he/she will only ask men to apply[35], not even considering to interview the few females who dared to react to the job advertisement. Factual or descriptive stereotypes may be quite accurate on a group level, but should nevertheless not be applied to judge individual human beings. In doing so, the stereotype will stand in the way of a woman's actual capacities or choices.[36]

A second category of descriptive stereotypes are those that do not have any empirical basis, but are purely based on prejudice, bias or stigma,[37] sometimes called 'false stereotypes'. E.g.: 'all blond women are stupid', or 'all fat women are lazy'. Most cultures are abundant in such stereotypes, often reproduced by

---

32 Cook & Cusack 2010, p 25.

33 Fiske et al. 1991.

34 The word factual is put between citation marks because we can never be certain in how far the actual conduct of women is not already determined by the expectations that gender stereotype have imposed on her. When a girl hears over and over again that women are no good in math and when her teacher has no confidence in her abilities in that field, she most probably will develop lesser math skills than her male class mates. Appiah 2000, p 49: "(...) there are obvious connections between statistical and normative stereotypes. Many of the generalizations involved in statistical stereotyping are true because there are normative stereotypes to which people are conforming."

35 Often implicitly, by means of using a male denominator of a particular job.

36 See for a more detailed description of the effects of stereotyping Fiske et al. 1991, p 1050–1051.

37 See Solanka 2008.

popular proverbs or sayings.[38] Although these stereotypes pretend to describe the true character of women, this description is not based an any evidence. Very often, these descriptions are pejorative, expressing the evilness, unreliability or badness of women. Even more than factual descriptive stereotypes, false stereotypes stand in the way of women's real capacities and free choices.

The second main characteristic of gender stereotypes is that through these (often implicit, subconscious) standard images of male and female human beings it is also *prescribed* what the proper male/female conduct in a particular culture and time is. Stereotypes very easily transgress from a description of (average statistical) facts to prescriptive norms. 'Most women prefer motherhood over job-career, therefore (all) women should stay at home to look after the children.' Or: 'Only women are able to give birth to children, therefore all women are destined to be and should act as mothers'. Meaning that they *should be* caring, putting their children first, nurturing, loving, and attentive; just to name a few of the most common prescriptive stereotypes that surround maternity and motherhood.[39] In that way, natural or biological differences between the sexes get a particular (often restrictive) meaning through culture.[40]

INVIDIOUS AND BENEVOLENT GENDER STEREOTYPES

Gender stereotypes should not be seen as bad in themselves. They play an important role in the construction of identity, be it on the individual level or on the level of a social group or nation. In personal identity formation, in any culture, being a girl or a boy makes a big difference. Girls and boys struggle with questions like: What clothes am I to wear? With what / whom am I to play? What kind of education is suitable for me? How do I relate to the other sex? Some struggle with the question in how far to follow the strict patterns of conduct that the community or society assigns to the biological sex that he/she (apparently) has, even if he/she feels differently about his/her gender identity. Gender stereotypes are ready made scripts for identities which are crucial for a human being to become a full member of the society or community.[41] These scripts can be positive or negative. According to the pejorative language of Article 5 CEDAW, not just any stereotyped representation of 'woman', or 'femaleness' should be modified, but only *social and cultural patterns of conduct* of men and women,

---

38 See Schippers 2005 for an extensive account of proverbial gender stereotypes all around the world.

39 Hernández-Truyol 2002, p 114/115.

40 Such natural differences between the sexes, therefore, to some degree are co-determined by nurture, i.e. by means of cultural prescriptions. This shows that an either-or-choice between 'nature' and 'nurture' is a human construct in itself.

41 Appiah 2000, p 52, and Appiah 1994.

and *prejudices and customary and all other practices*, which are based on *stereotyped roles for men and women* and *ideas about the inferiority or superiority of either of the sexes*. The Convention thereby only refers to gender stereotypes that are invidious or harmful for women.[42] It is therefore necessary to examine whether a gender stereotype plays a role in the construction of social, economic, cultural and legal *inequality* between men and women, or leads to *subordination* of women and violates the principles of women's equality and dignity.[43]

The usage of the word 'invidious' in relation to gender stereotypes can lead to the suggestion that some stereotypes which are favourable for women – sometimes called 'benevolent stereotypes'[44] – are ok and should be left alone. Nice gestures and pleasantries from men towards women (and *vice versa*) should not be subjected to change. Also, views in which it is expressed that women are more oriented towards personal relations, that they are more caring, or are more able to preserve and nurture the earth, may appear to be positive, instead of invidious. However, the effect of such stereotypes, often is "(...) that exposure to benevolent sexist views held by others increases the extent to which women self-define in relational terms, decreases the degree to which they view themselves in task-related terms, and diminishes their leadership aspirations."[45] Although seemingly very nice or respectful, the result of such benevolent stereotypes may be that they keep women in their place.

FIXED PARENTAL GENDER ROLES; THE CONSTRUCTION OF GENDER IN/THROUGH THE FAMILY

Crucial in the construction of women's inferiority, subordination and/or difference, is her sexuality[46], her reproductive capacity and her nurturing and caring role as regards her children, her husband and the wider family.[47] In this role women are not only the birthmothers of the next generations, but are also in charge of reproducing the group's culture; they not only feed their children with the meals that they prepare, but also with the norms, practices, values, beliefs and traditions, that are crucial for the social group's or nation's identity. "The

42 See Appiah 2000, p 43. The Committee sometimes speaks of 'adverse cultural norms'. E.g. CO Madagascar, CEDAW/C/MDG/CO/5 (2008) para. 16.
43 Appiah 2000, p 44.
44 Baretto & Ellemers 2005.
45 Baretto et al. 2009.
46 In sexuality women are seen as 'passive' or 'receptive', but also as 'seductive'. Women are to be protected from 'male aggressiveness' in sexual affairs, but also from their own 'seductive' nature. Historically, there is a strong reason for the control of women's sexuality: men need to be absolutely sure that the children are theirs; which justifies a strict sexual ethical code for women in many cultures.
47 See e.g. Chodorow 1989.

point is that reproduction is of fundamental importance to the (continued) existence of nations – 'populate or perish' – and women are entrusted with the task of providing new members."[48]

Gender relations thus are seen as constituting the essence of a particular culture, to be passed by women from generation to generation.[49] This so-called *natural* female role in many cultures serves at the ultimate excuse to keep women in their place, i.e. in the safe haven of the male controlled family. "The story of gender in traditionalist cultures and religions is that of the systematic domination of women by men, of women's exclusion from public power, and of their subjection to patriarchal power within the family."[50] Although the content of the *prejudices and customary and all other practices*, to which Article 5(a) CEDAW refers, may differ widely between the various regions and cultures in the world, "[T]he most globally pervasive of the harmful practices (...) is the stereotyping of women exclusively as mothers and housewives in a way that limits their opportunities to participate in public life, whether political or economical."[51] In that way, the construction of male and female gender identities amounts to a fixation of the 'appropriate' or 'natural' roles for each of the two genders. The subsequent Article 5(b) CEDAW therefore calls for revealing and breaking open these fixed parental gender roles and enhancing the opportunities for women and men to share responsibilities as regards the upbringing of their children.

The fact that the construction of gender relations is very strongly connected to the construction of the traditional family, means that changing gender identities of individual men and women can not be separated from changing the way in which the family is constructed. Very often it can be heard that equality of women is not the right norm because this would undermine the family.[52] And family, in turn, is seen as the cornerstone of society.[53] Women's role in reproduction and in the family therefore is a very strong social norm, which can not be changed by (individual) women alone.[54]

---

48 Van den Brink 2008, p 77, referring to McClintock 1993, at. p. 61.

49 Ibid.

50 Raday 2007, p 69.

51 Raday 2007, p 71.

52 Complementarity or equity are then suggested as alternatives. See below in the next sub-paragraph.

53 The form the family takes may differ, e.g. the extended family, women headed families or the (Western) 'core-family' existing of a heterosexual couple and children.

54 See Mackie & LeJeune 2009. See also Report of the UN Secretary General, *'The Girl Child'*, UN Doc A/64/315, 31 August 2009, paras 64 and 68.

WOMEN'S INHERENTLY DIFFERENT ROLE: NOT EQUAL RIGHTS BUT EQUAL IN DIGNITY

As with gender stereotypes, it is possible to distinguish between gender roles that are more or less damaging or obstacles for the realisation of women's human rights. In this respect, there are many forms of attributing different roles to men and women of which at first sight it is not obvious that they are detrimental for women. For a long time it has been seen as benevolent that women were exempted from the draft and did not have to go to war and get themselves killed; their role was to send their sons to the battle fields. Also exemptions from night work and from certain kinds of dangerous work (e.g. in mining or in nuclear industry) were greeted by many people (women included) as a blessing. In many countries a form of secular and state controlled reproduction of the patriarchal system takes place when women are being conceived of as in need of protection by means of special legal and policy measures, mainly with regard to childbirth and motherhood. This protection, however, is offered in such a way that women's human rights (most importantly the right to be economically active and financially independent) are severely restricted. Men, in the same systems, are seen as head of the household or as the breadwinner, and on that ground regarded as deserving rights in the area of economic subsistence by the State.[55] However, such regulations may appear to be a mixed blessing since they may take away opportunities for women to be involved in those particular areas of life, and to play an active part in changing the conditions of life. This is particularly so, when the exclusion of women affects their political and economic participation.

In many patriarchal stories about gender relations, women are not seen as inferior, but as inherently different from men.[56] Not equality between men and women, but men and women being complementary and equal in dignity and worth is then the leading principle. Instead of equality, the term 'equity' is often being used to express the nature of the relations between the sexes. Statements to this effect can be found in many States parties' contributions in the constructive dialogue with the CEDAW Committee. For example: "The representative stated that the notions of the role of women in the family should not be changed. A misunderstanding of equality would not benefit any society. It was more important to encourage the idea of the complementarity of men and women."[57] Occasionally in patriarchal stories about the 'true' relationship between the sexes 'woman' is seen as superior to 'man', especially with respect to her caring or nurturing capacities. 'Woman' thus is put on a high pedestal, i.e. as deserving a

[55] See para. 2.4, where we describe that the CEDAW Committee often has expressed its concerns in this respect.
[56] See our discussion about 'nature' or 'nurture' above.
[57] CO Guatemala, UN Doc.A/49/38, 13th Session (1994) para. 68.

special degree of respect and concern[58] of men, of civil society and/or of the government.

GENDER STEREOTYPES AND INTERSECTIONAL DISCRIMINATION

However, a woman gets this sacred position and respect and concern only when and in as far as she obliges to fulfil the traditionally, customary or religiously determined duties that come along with primarily or exclusively being a mother/caregiver. The other side of celebrating women's 'relational orientation' or her 'special nurturing capacities' is that every transgression of her gender identity or gender role is legally impossible or inconceivable because basic legal concepts exclude women and women's experiences[59], and/or are severely punished in social life or in the family, even to the extent of being killed. The most blatant transgression of the patriarchal female gender identity and her fixed gender (motherly) role is the lesbian woman who chooses to denounce a male sexual partner and thereby also rejects the protection of the male head of household, and all other forms of male supervision on and control of her life.[60] Therefore, gender stereotypes and fixed parental gender roles directly affect the lives of lesbian women as well as of gay men, who denounce the traditional male role.[61] The identity or role of 'man' in the patriarchal system is that of the person in charge of maintaining and preserving this 'natural order' and preventing that 'his' woman (wife, sister, daughter, or any other female relative) cast a shadow of shame on the family. It is not to be forgotten that also males who do not oblige to gender stereotypes and fixed parental gender roles bring shame upon the family or community and may be punished socially and/or legally. The construction of gender relations therefore is also oppressive for men who deviate from their traditional gender role, as well as for transsexual people, intersexual people and homosexual people. Through the mechanism of gender stereotyping, discrimination on the ground of sexual orientation and discrimination of

---

58 See the works of legal philosopher Ronald Dworkin (most notably in his *Taking Rights Seriously*). According to Dworkin the fundamental principle of equality means 'equal respect and concern', i.e. relevant differences between individuals are attended to (most notably by the State) in an appropriate way, thereby guaranteeing *de facto* equality between them. However, in many traditionalist cultures and religions, the respect and concern that women 'deserve' on the basis of their biological capacity of childbearing and their traditional role in child rearing, is not based on the notion of equality but on the notion of equity.

59 See Smart 1989 and Smart 1992, and Holtmaat 2004, p 87.

60 Lesbian women being gang raped in order 'to cure her' from her outrageous 'abnormal' sexual preference, is an example of this kind of 'corrections'. See g. Report of the UN Special Rapporteur on the question of torture and other cruel, inhuman or degrading treatment or punishment, Commission on Human Rights, March 2006, UN Doc. E/CN.4/2006/6/Add.1, paras 180 and 183.

61 Cook & Cusack 2010, p 2.

transsexual and intersexual people intersects[62] with discrimination on the ground of sex and – from the perspective of Article 5 CEDAW – should be eliminated and combated by all States.[63] A transformation of gender and of compulsory heterosexuality needs to take place simultaneously.[64]

Gender stereotyping may also intersect with a wide range of other identities that are created or constructed in the social, legal and cultural life of any given society, like for example the fixed and stereotypical identity of a *divorcee*, a *single woman*, a *childless woman*, a *housewife*, a *working mother*, a *welfare mother*, a *widow*, a *battered woman*, an *immigrant woman*, an *indigenous woman*, a *rural woman*, a *woman of colour*, a *prostitute*, or a *criminal woman*.[65] This means that other factors than a woman's biological sex co-determine the descriptive and prescriptive stereotypes that to a large extent determine the conditions of her life. Economic position, class or caste, religion, sexual orientation, legal status, health, age, social status, nationality, ethnic origin or 'race', all lie at the basis of discrimination sustained by stereotypes that combine and intersect with gender stereotypes.[66] The CEDAW Committee acknowledges that certain groups of women "in addition to being affected by gender stereotypes, face multiple forms of discrimination, on grounds such as their ethnicity or their sexual orientation".[67]

GENDER STEREOTYPES AND FIXED PARENTAL GENDER ROLES AS UNIVERSAL PHENOMENA

It should be remembered that Article 5 CEDAW contains a norm that is applicable in all States that signed up this Convention. As is shown by the

62 Crenshaw 1989. Related terms are 'compounded discrimination', or 'multiple discrimination'.

63 The Committee recognises that women may be discriminated on the ground of their sexuality, thereby possibly including their homosexuality. However, it seems to be hesitant to use that word or to use the word lesbianism. See e.g. CO Guatemala, CEDAW/C/GUA/CO7 (2009) para. 19, where it speaks of sexuality in general. It has mentioned sexual orientation and gender identity in CO Panama, CEDAW/C/PAN/CO/7 (2010) para. 22.

64 Gross 2008, p 252.

65 See Smart 1992, who discusses the legal construction of the 'bad mother'.

66 See e.g. *Yilmaz-Dogan v. the Netherlands*, CERD Committee, Communication of 10 August 1988, CERD/C/36/D/1/1984, for a case of intersection between gender and racial/ethnic stereotyping.

67 Sexuality: CO Guatemala, CEDAW/C/GUA/CO7 (2009) para. 19; sexual orientation and gender identity: CO Panama, CEDAW/C/PAN/CO/7 (2010) para. 22; minority or immigrant status: CO New Zealand, CEDAW/C/NZL/CO/6 (2007) para. 22; CO France, CEDAW/C/FRA/CO/6 (2008) para. 18; CO The Netherlands, CEDAW/C/NLD/CO/5 (2010) para. 24; CO Cyprus, CEDAW/C/CYP/CO/5 (2006) para. 31; Roma women: CO Hungary, CEDAW/C/EST/HUN/CO/6 (2007) para. 31; CO Romania, CEDAW/C/ROM/06 (2006) paras 26, 27; widows: CO Nepal, UN DOC.A/59/38, 31st Session (2004) para. 206; rural women: CO Camaroon, CEDAW/C/CMR/CO/3 (2009) para. 42.

comments of the CEDAW Committee, not one single culture in today's world is completely free from gender stereotypes and fixed parental gender roles. These phenomena are based in traditions which are as old as human life itself. According to this earth's patriarchal stories 'woman's' very existence is dependent upon or is derived from 'man'. This is reflected in numerous antique myths about the way in which humankind came into being / was created. Exemplary are the creationist stories in the founding texts of the three big monotheist religions, the Old Testament and the Koran. During the long history of humanity – with the rare exception of a few matriarchal cultures – 'woman' has always been and is persistently being constructed as 'the other', that is: as *not-a-man*.[68]

The construction of gender stereotypes and fixed parental gender roles ultimately rests upon the assumption that there are two *opposite* and mutually *exclusive* biological sexes. At the basis of this binary construction lies a *hierarchy* of the two sexes: 'woman' being the negative or inferior side of the two poles, thereby justifying male domination over her. Patriarchy and misogyny are of all times and of all places. This includes today (A.D. 2010) and the world's most women-friendly societies. As the motto of this Chapter explains: it is not a matter of distinguishing between patriarchal and non-patriarchal societies, it is a matter of recognising that societies are *differently patriarchal*. The same applies to different communities within a particular country, for example between rural and urban areas, or between the cultures of different ethnic groups within a country. Thus, within a country, various subcultures may coexist concurrently. The diverse and sometimes contradictory normative systems provide the rationale for varied patterns of gender roles and identities, indicating different power relations. Gender equality may be accepted conceptually in some subcultures while 'old fashioned patriarchy' prevails in others.[69] All this variety may be used to exemplify that gender hierarchy or gender inequality is a social construct, and not something that stems from human nature as such or from a God-given order.

THE (IM)POSSIBILITY TO MODIFY GENDER STEREOTYPES AND FIXED PARENTAL GENDER ROLES

Abolishing, eradicating or eliminating[70] gender stereotypes and fixed parental gender roles, or even *modifying* them, is a very difficult enterprise. The main reason why change is so difficult to achieve has to do with the fact that stereotypes fulfil three main functions in human life: (1) they maximise simplicity and

68 De Beauvoir 1952.

69 Raday 2003, p 665–666.

70 This language was used in first drafts of Article 5 CEDAW.

predictability, (2) they assign difference between classes or groups of people, and (3) they construct social or cultural identities.[71] The first function means that gender stereotypes serve as a prediction of what kind of behaviour you may expect from a woman or a man. As such they fulfil an important cognitive function: "[S]tereotypes provide structure and meaning, and they shape perceptions most when the data themselves are open to multiple interpretations, (…)."[72] The second function is based on the cognitive structure of the human mind, in which it is easiest to learn things when they fit into dichotomized pairs of concepts[73]; a system of fixed classifications helps us to construct such pairs. The pair 'female' and 'male' is closely connected to many other pairs of concepts, like e.g. warm-cold, dark-light, emotional-rational, soft-hard, et cetera. The construction of such 'essential' differences between male and female is also closely related to sexuality or sexual attractiveness (to the other or to the same sex).[74] In the third place (as we have already discussed above), stereotypes play an important function in the construction of identity, be it on the individual level or on the level of a social group or nation. Abolishing gender stereotypes would mean that the basis of this identity would be taken away, which would most certainly lead to an identity crisis; this in turn leads to great anxiety, something most people try to avoid at all costs.

Gender stereotypes are also very difficult to change because they form part of what human beings experience as their natural environment, which means that they are not recognised as such.[75] Gender stereotypes are so deeply inscribed in our language, images, practices, norms, values, et cetera, that we are hardly aware of the fact that we continuously use them in our interactions with other people. As was described earlier in this Chapter, they are often vested deeply in our subconscious, and can only be brought to light with the help of psychological tests, such as the *Implicit Association Test*. Therefore, any strategy to overcome or to modify them should start with revealing the constructed (cultural) nature of stereotyped (unequal) gender relations, by clarifying that they to a large extent are not natural but man made. Visibility only occurs when certain so-called natural or eternal practices or beliefs are confronted with other practices or

71 Cook & Cusack 2010, p 14–20.

72 Fiske et al. 1991, p 1050.

73 These pairs are always opposed to each other: black- white, good-bad, girl-boy, day-night, emotional-rational, etc. One part of the pair often denotes something positive, the other something negative.

74 Appiah 2000, p 43.

75 Hofstadter 1995. See also Cook & Cusack 2010, p 179. Stereotypes are invisible because they surround us. Hofstadter uses the metaphor of fish that swim in the deep see: as long as they have never surfaced they will not be aware of the fact that they are surrounded by water. For such awareness it is necessary to be able to observe that water is different from air.

beliefs in other human societies.[76] For example: when a culture holds it to be true that women who have given birth to a child for that reason are not capable to work for at least some months (and therefore – for their own safety and good – are prohibited to work in that period of time), people may come to understand that this is cultural instead of natural when confronted with societies where women are back at work a few hours after delivery.

A final reason why gender stereotypes and fixed parental gender roles are very difficult to change, is that they are embedded in strong social norms. A characteristic of such norms is that it is very difficult for an individual or even for one family, to adopt practices or behaviour that contravenes them: "The continuation or the abandonment of each practice involves a set of social rewards and punishments and operates as what is known in social science as a social norm. The theory argues that each practice is a community practice that must be ended by the whole community coordinating its abandonment (...)."[77] With respect to female genital mutilation, for example, as a practice that is related to the marriageability of girls, it is quite impossible for just one family to give up this practice, let alone for just one individual woman or girl: "What one family chooses to do depends upon what other families in that community choose to do. No one family has an incentive to deviate: if they do, their daughter is destined not to be married or to have a poor marriage."[78] It is only possible to give up the practice *together*.[79]

For the reasons discussed above, it is not realistic to set as a policy aim to *eradicate*, *eliminate* or *abolish* all gender stereotypes and fixed parental gender roles; the purpose can only be to *transform* or to *modify* those stereotypes and roles that are obstacles for the realisation of women's human rights. The most harmful practices that are based on unequal gender relations should be targeted first in such programmes, realising that any such cultural reform will be slow and difficult to achieve. However, such reform initiatives "(...) could begin to make it less true that our society constructs women as inferior to men."[80]

---

76 See also Nyamu 2000, p 413, who states that making available empirical evidence of cultural variation is of crucial importance for enhancing any process of cultural change.

77 Mackie & LeJeune 2009, p V.

78 Mackie & LeJeune, p 10. See also Report of the UN Secretary General, *'The Girl Child'*, UN Doc A/64/315, 31 August 2009, paras 64 and 68.

79 This reasoning has led to developing various sorts of Community Empowerment Programmes where a group of families enrol in sensitisation training programmes and then share knowledge with others. When the critical majority of families within one community is reached all other families easily follow. See UNFPA's Technical Report of their Global Consultation on FGM/C, held in July 2007, for many examples of successful elimination of the practice of FGM/C.

80 Appiah 2000, p 52.

3.3 ESSENTIALIST APPROACHES TO CULTURE AND GENDER

The way in which culture is conceptualised determines how social and cultural change is imagined. If culture is regarded as fixed and unchanging, it is a barrier that needs to be removed or abolished, for example through education or through international pressure. If culture is seen as a set of practices and meanings which are shaped by institutional, economic and social contexts, it is both malleable and embedded in structures of power; it could then be changed when effective 'counter power' strategies are employed. These different perspectives on culture deeply affect policies concerning women's human rights.[81] A most important obstacle to cultural change and changing persistent unequal gender relations, is the widely held belief of cultural essentialism, which in turn is closely related to seeing gender as something static and immutable.[82] Or, as Yakin Ertürk has put it in her 2007 report on the intersection between culture and violence against women:

> "Essentialized interpretation of culture are used either to justify violation of women's rights in the name of culture or to categorically condemn cultures 'out there' as being inherently primitive and violent towards women. Both variants of cultural essentialism ignore the universal dimensions of patriarchal culture that subordinates, albeit differently, women in all societies and fails to recognize women's active agency in resisting and negotiating culture to improve their terms of existence."[83]

CULTURAL ESSENTIALISM

The term 'cultural essentialism' refers to approaches in which it is taken as a fact that each and every culture on earth possesses distinctive inherent and essential features ('essences') which belong or adhere to that particular culture.[84] Such approaches represent different cultures as if they were *natural phenomena*, i.e. as entities that exist and have always existed, neatly distinct and separated from

---

81 Merry 2006, p 15.

82 As Merry (2003 Polar) argues, often advocates of women's human rights adhere to such a static and essentialists view of culture, thereby ignoring more modern trends in cultural anthropology in which this stance has long been replaced by theories in which culture is being seen as fluid and dynamic.

83 UN Special Rapporteur on VAW, 'Intersections between culture and violence against women'; 17 January 2007, UN Doc. A/HRC/4/34, para. 68.

84 The term essentialism refers to an epistemological approach in which it is presumed that we are able to capture the essence of 'beings' (phenomena or things/beings that we can observe) by means of giving a fixed description of them. This is opposed to the understanding of culture and gender as something that not 'is', but that is constantly being produced and reproduced (also by the process of research and description itself!), as being *fluid* and a *process*. See Gherardi 1994.

each other. Most often, this is expressed by means of speaking of '*the* ... culture'. For example: '*the* Dutch culture', '*the* culture of India', '*the* Buddhist culture'.[85] This picture tends to obscure the fact that the boundaries between cultures are fluid and – as far as they exist – are themselves human constructs. Such boundaries are embedded in and deployed for a variety of personal, institutional and political reasons and purposes. Essentialist representations of culture conceal the fact that the *labels* that are used to demarcate or individuate particular cultures themselves have a historical provenance, and that what they declare as distinctive features of a particular culture has changed over time.[86] Rather, such articulations of the presumed *true* character of a particular culture should be understood as competing efforts to preserve certain social, economic, and political arrangements, i.e. to preserve the *status quo.* As such they are expressions of existing power relations between or within certain groups or societies. Often only the dominant voices within a particular cultural community are in the position to declare that such essential cultural characteristics would indeed exist and, as is often added immediately, are more true or are superior to any other culture.[87] Or, from the perspective of the 'other' culture: to see a particular culture as 'backward', 'evil' or 'pre-modern'.

GENDER ESSENTIALISM

There exists a similar essentialist approach to gender and gender relations, which is often closely linked to cultural essentialism. In the same way as happens with culture, one can hear people speak about fixed and eternal characteristics of 'woman', or 'man'.[88] As soon as the existing (unequal) relations between men and women are being seen as purely natural, as God-given, as reflecting the essential characteristics of male and female human beings, or as belonging to a *given* culture, they become *eternal* and *unchangeable.*[89] The aim and obligation of modifying gender stereotypes and fixed parental gender roles, as has been laid down in Article 5 CEDAW, thereby becomes impossible or even revolutionary, in the sense of contravening the natural or eternal God-given order of human

85 Using the singular article 'the' means that it is presumed that there is *only one* such culture, leaving no space for different interpretations, or differences between members of that culture. Opening up space for differentiation is seen as very threatening. Compare the commotion around the Dutch Princess Maxima's statement that there is no such thing as '*the* Dutch culture' or '*the* Dutch identity'. Speech held at 24 September 2007; see for a description of the emotional reactions to her statement the introduction to the 2008 report of the Sociaal Cultureel Planbureau on Social Cohesion (Dutch only) to be found at: www.scp.nl/dsresource ?objectid=19744&type=org.

86 Narayan 1998, p 92.

87 Nyamu 2000, 405–406.

88 In Dutch: '*de* vrouw' and '*de* man'.

89 See Narayan 1998.

relations. Traditionalists or fundamentalist cultures often are inclined to take such an essentialist stance towards gender and denounce any international obligations to eliminate discrimination of women.

Essentialist approaches to culture and gender, however, are not only to be found among spokespersons of fundamentalist religions or traditionalist communities, but also among those who defend an 'abolitionist', a 'post modern', 'anti-colonialist', or 'cultural relativist' standpoint. All such approaches tend to depart from a *static*, instead of from a *dynamic* conceptualisation of culture and gender and therefore to make it impossible to have a fruitful dialogue about the issue of cultural change. For this reason, we describe here by whom and why such essentialists approaches are being voiced in contemporary debates about women's human rights and culture. We first discuss some important internal essentialist perspectives; the external ones come at the end of this paragraph.

BENEFICIARIES OF MAINTAINING THE STATUS QUO (INTERNAL PERSPECTIVES)

It is understandable that those people who benefit from features of a particular culture in which women are seen as inferior to men and are subordinated to male power will try to defend these features as being essential, and therefore being immutable. As Florence Butegwa observes: "African women and men need to join others who actively wonder and ask why it is only when women want to bring about change for their own benefit do culture and custom become sacred and unchangeable."[90] Those who benefit from the patriarchal gender system are in power and powerful people will not yield power happily nor easily. As such we distinguish five main stakeholders in maintaining the *status quo* of women's inequality: *individual men* and *individual women* who are members of a particular culture, *families*, male *leaders of traditionalist communities* or organisations and institutions, and *the State* itself.

Individual men's resistance against changing unequal gender relations

Individual men greatly benefit from the strict gender division that exists in many cultures. When women are confined to the private sphere doing all the hard and time consuming work that is needed for the reproduction of human kind, this leaves ample space for men to exercise power over them on the personal, social, economical and political level. Men have a lot to gain from an essentialist approach to culture and gender. Fear of losing their culturally defined dominant role (and therefore: fear of losing their culturally designed and defined

90 Butegwa 2002, p 123.

masculinity) may effectively barrier any real change in favour of women. This resistance is not always caused by bad will of men. They actually might be unaware of the suffering of women, precisely because they are used to regarding men and women as unequal. That is what they have been brought up with.[91] Or as the renowned American philosopher Martha Nussbaum observes: "We have hardly begun to take the measure of the full weight of habit, family and community pressures, and the sheer fear of change, when we think of about how men who are not basically evil or sadistic frequently resist such changes, while believing that they do treat women as ends."[92]

In order to achieve fundamental changes of unequal gender relations, it is not enough that women be empowered and take the course of their lives (more) in their own hands; for that, men need to change as well. This requires that men take on a new male identity, one that many men may perceive of as less powerful or less sexual attractive. Women who start exercising their human rights, will unavoidably contest and undermine the existing traditional male gender identity. An example of this problem is to be found in the work of Sally Engle Merry. From a series of interviews with battering men, it appeared that most of these men talked about shock, anger, surprise and a sense of betrayal by the women who had turned to the legal system to protect them. For the first time in their lives, these men had been resisted and rejected by a woman, and as a consequence of that experienced a diminished self; they felt not heard by the judiciary, humiliated and ignored, and were subjected to penalties, all of which was a completely new and severely destabilising experience for most of them.[93]

Women as defenders of culture and existing gender relations

A second category of stakeholders in essentialist and static perceptions of culture and gender are women who are members of particular cultures. Similar to men, the personal identity of women to a high degree is determined by gender stereotypes that describe and prescribe what it means to be a 'real' or a 'good' woman. Women most notably withhold themselves to stand up for their human rights because this requires a major shift in their own gendered personal identity. With respect to battered women, Sally Engle Merry states that, despite considerable emphasis on their rights by staff members of shelters and by lawyers working for the courts or the public prosecutor's office, battered women are slow to see themselves as bearers of rights. They clearly fear retaliation by the

91 See above, where we have discussed that gender stereotypes have the appearance of being 'natural' and function at the subconscious level, and thus become invisible.

92 Nussbaum 2000, p 162. Her last observation relates to the (Kantian) human rights value that human beings should be treated as ends in themselves, not as means for achieving other people's purposes. See para. 2.1.

93 Merry 2003, p 355.

perpetrator, but they also resist the shift in subjectivity which is by required the law. "Taking on a rights-defined self in relation to a partner requires a substantial identity change both for the woman and for the man she is accusing. Instead of seeing herself defined by family, kin and work relationships, she takes on a more autonomous self protected by the state."[94] When turning to a rights-approach, a battered woman may be pressured by kin to feel she is a bad wife, while her partner may claim she is taking away his masculinity.

This is clearly a very difficult situation to master for most women, let alone for women who have been subjected to (sexual) violence by their own partner, from whom most of them often are not only emotionally but also economically dependent. Any adult person who is asked to cast away a firmly entrenched culturally defined understanding of his or her own personal (gender) identity may encounter serious existentialist anxieties. The easiest way for women to 'opt out' of programmes that are aimed at enhancing their human rights and achieving more equality, is to state that their culture in essence contravenes women's equality, that their culture in essence is good for them, or that their obedience to cultural norms and practices is their own free choice.[95] Programmes that do not recognise these resistances to change and the difficulties that women who dare to propose such change encounter, most probably will not be effective in achieving any real progress. Women certainly need examples from brave women within their own culture:

> "When we make videos, and women like us watch them, we get confidence to try and make changes. When we see women like us who have done something brave and new, then we get confidence that we can learn something new too. When poor women see other poor women as health workers on the video, they say, 'I can also learn about health and help solve these problems in my neighbourhood'."[96]

The family's interest to maintain unequal gender relations

A third category of stakeholders in defending the status quo with a call on culture are families. Of course, families consist of men and women and often encompass more than two generations of them; however, it is the family as a unity (perhaps with internal conflicting interests, but externally acting in unison) that we refer to here. Families have great interest in raising their offspring in such a way that their position within the wider community is maintained. For example: when a family is known as 'bad', this means that the children's opportunities to marry and to start their own family and their position within

94 Merry 2003, p 345.

95 In Chapter 4, para. 4.3 we deal with the issue of choice in more detail.

96 Lila Datania, SEWA, Ahmedabad, India 1992, as quoted in Nussbaum 2000, p 111, derived from Rose, *Where women are leaders*, p 158.

the community is affected. The construction of the gendered and heterosexual family with its fixed unequal and divided gender roles amounts to what social scientists call the construction of a social norm, which can only be changed when the whole community is prepared to adopt new norms and practices.[97] Religion, custom and tradition have a great influence on what is perceived as a 'proper' family. However, this constructed family is not only a culturally effective social norm, it is a social norm that is also firmly entrenched in a whole range of *legal* and *formal institutional* arrangements in all societies. In many societies, including in the West, family is seen as the cornerstone of society. *Family law*, therefore, is an important 'battlefield' when it comes down to the process of modifying gender relations.[98] For that reason, it does not come as a surprise that most reservations to CEDAW are made to the Articles 2 and 16 in which the right to legal equality of women in family law is laid down.

Male leadership's resistance against a democratisation of culture

Male leadership of traditional and religious communities organisations, or institutions also will not easily give in to a change in the prevailing gender relations, because such a development will most certainly also entail a change of the rules of who governs these communities or institutions. Very often, most notably in religious communities, but also in tribal ethnic or social groups, it is only (elderly or 'priestly') men who are eligible of becoming a leader.[99] As soon as women's equal right to co-determine what exactly is the essence of their culture is implemented, women may decide that this essence is different from the way male leadership has always portrayed it, and may wish to redefine it. For male leadership a process of democratisation of culture therefore entails a most eminent danger to their position of power over the community or society.

The State's resistance to loosen its gendered construction of national identity

There is yet a fifth group of stakeholders in maintaining the *status quo* of unequal gender relations. The construction of a particular cultural specificity to a high degree may influence a State's perception of its *essential national identity* through which it distinguishes itself from other States. This is particularly true for governments of nations that have to find a new post colonial identity, or that are

97 See above, where we discussed the work of Mackie & LeJeune 2009.

98 In respect to the gendered construction of heterosexuality, the exclusion of same sex couples from the right to marry under most family laws is exemplary.

99 Compare the declaration of the Pope of the Catholic Church, in July 2010, that it is *a serious crime* when women perform priestly functions within that church. (See: www.standaard.be/artikel/detail.aspx?artikelid=N32SUGIR; last accessed on July 28, 2010). There are some examples of case law where women have successfully contested such rules. See e.g. the South African Constitutional Court case of *Shilubana and Others v. Nwamitwa*, 2007 (2) SA 432. See www.saflii.org/za/cases/ZACC/2008/9.html (last accessed on July 28, 2010).

kept together by the artificial construction of a particular 'own' and 'unique' national cultural identity, thereby in fact covering severe ethnic, social and/or economic differences within the country.[100] The use of nation-building myths, historical heroes, national hymns, national symbols, et cetera, often has discriminatory side-effects, and may be used as an excuse for violence against those who do not truly 'belong' within the nation, or against those who advocate for a fundamental change of the nation's culture. Time and again those holding governmental powers feel in need of explicitly framing the country's national identity in terms of a fixed set of proclaimed cultural features, often in order to legitimise their rule. Their culture is then perceived as the 'national essence', and this essence becomes fundamental to claims of internal and external sovereignty and ethno-nationalism.

It is important to recognise the strong link between national identity and gender. The construction of stereotyped gender identities and fixed parental gender roles very much lies at the basis of the claimed specific or unique identity of many (traditionalist) cultures, which are adopted and presented as a *national* culture. These (presumed) essential national cultural characteristics notably often include national / cultural myths about the ideal woman.[101] National identities often coalesce around women's bodies and incorporate racial or ethnic judgements.[102] Therefore, States may have a great interest in maintaining the existing (unequal) gendered social and cultural order. To a high degree such culture is expressed in culture specific rules and practices with respect to how women should behave, and which deny women's equality and curtail women's freedoms. These rules or practices are not just expressions of oppression or hatred of women, but serve to preserve and sustain the nation's particular cultural or religious *identity* or even its very existence. Quite often, a State in its Constitution recognises the validity or priority of certain religious or customary laws, mainly in the area of family relations[103], and on that basis has made a reservation to the CEDAW Convention.[104] Such laws are officially recognised and exempted from the (also Constitutional) non-discrimination norms.[105] Sometimes a government goes as

---

100 In fact most nations have been constructed in that way. Examples are the extensive 'nation building' activities of newly established 'national entities' like Italy, France and Germany in the 18th and 19th Century.

101 Most famous in this respect are two crucial symbols of cultural unity in France, consisting of the images of two women: Jeanne D'Arc and Marianne.

102 Volpp, 2000, p 90.

103 An example of a 'modern' State where this is the case, is Israel. See Raday 2008.

104 Reservations that are made on the ground of respect for damaging religious or customary laws are not recognised by the Committee. See e.g. CO Israel CEDAW/C/ISR/CO/3 (2005) para. 25; and CO India, CEDAW/C/IND/CO/3 (2007) para. 10.

105 See e.g. CO Botswana, CEDAW/C/BOT/CO/3 (2010) para. 23. On the basis of Articles 5 and/ or 2(f), the Committee rejects direct discrimination of women that flows from the official recognition of religious or customary laws. E.g. CO Burundi, CEDAW/C/BDI/CO/4 (2008) para. 13; CO Vanuatu, CEDAW/C/VUT/CO/3 (2007) para. 10; CO Namibia, CEDAW/C/

far as proclaiming that the prevailing gender relations within the family form "the foundation of the State".[106] In some instances traditional gender relations are embedded in the State's Constitution, in order for the State to distinguish itself from other States (e.g. from a State from which it has become independent, after a long duration of colonisation). Exemplary for this is the Irish Constitution, which, according to the CEDAW Committee, reflects a stereotyped image of the roles of women "in the home and as mothers".[107]

DEMONIZING CULTURE[108] OR MAKING IT IMMUNE TO CRITICISM (EXTERNAL PERSPECTIVES)

A different stream of arguments that are based on essentialist and static perceptions of culture and gender does not come from inside particular cultures (as was discussed above), but are voiced by some advocates for women's human rights. We have found three different manifestations of this position.

Orientalising culture

In academic and policy/political discourses about the difficulties surrounding the implementation of international human rights standards in the area of women's human rights, often a sharp divide is being constructed between 'global legal standards' and 'local culture'. In this framework it is concluded that international human rights norms proclaim the idea and ideal of equality between women and men, but that all around the world domestic or local cultural ideas and practices are stubbornly rejecting these norms. In this divide, culture is seen as something that exists locally, not on the international level itself. It therefore does not recognise that accepting and promoting international human rights standards, including their particular humanistic value basis (see para. 2.1), is also part of the construction of human culture. In the words of Sally Engle Merry: This divide does not acknowledge that there exists something like a 'culture of human rights', and a 'culture of transnational modernity'.[109] Culture is being placed 'out there'.

NAM/CO/3 (2007) para. 16; CO Niger, CEDAW/C/NER/CO/2 (2007) para. 15; CO Indonesia, CEDAW/C/EST/IDN/CO/5 (2007) para. 12.

106 CO Guatemala, UN Doc.A/49/38, 13th Session (1994) para. 70.

107 CO Ireland, UN Doc.A/54/38, 21st Session (1999) paras 193–194. The Committee here refers to Article 41(2) of the Irish Constitution. Catholic Ireland thus wanted to distinguish itself from protestant Britain. See Van den Brink 2008.

108 Terminology derived from Merry 2003 Polar.

109 Merry 2006, p 16.

Implicitly, however, this humanistic cultural value basis is being recognised, since not all local cultures are deemed to be so stubbornly rejecting women's human rights. The rejection of the idea of women's equality is said to mainly take place within some 'other' cultures; meaning: in cultures that are 'alien' to the Western 'enlightened' value orientation. The very *essence* of such 'other' cultures, religions, customs or traditions is then constructed as 'non-enlightened', 'pre-modern', 'primitive', or 'traditional'. In the international human rights discourse the notion of culture is often equated with (mainly 'bad') traditions that exist 'out there' in rural areas and in primitive villages. Anthropologist Sally Engle Merry observes that labelling a culture as 'traditional' evokes an evolutionary vision of change from a primitive form of human life, to something like civilisation, similar to the vision of earlier colonial imperialism.[110] Culture in this sense is not used to describe the affluent countries of the global North or West, but only the poor countries in the global South, particularly isolated and rural villages and minority communities where life is understood by seemingly fixed customary practices and traditional views. Sally Engle Merry continues: "As I observed UN meetings, I found that transnational elite's often located culture 'out there' in villages and rural areas rather than 'in here' in their offices and conference rooms. Culture more often describes the developing world than the developed one."[111] Western subjects are thus defined by their ability to freely determine the course of their lives, in contrast to non-western subjects, who are defined by their group-based determinism. In fact, this is deeply dehumanising, because it denies subjects 'elsewhere' (outside the protected and affluent societies of Western human rights activists) the human capacity of agency and the ability to make rational choices about the course of their lives.[112]

This discourse is sometimes called 'orientalising culture'.[113] In it, particular 'other' (i.e. non-Western) cultures are seen as static, monolithic entities with a certain essence, that in the name of women's human rights need to be changed (if necessary with external force); or even better: to be completely eradicated or abolished. This process is particularly visible in international and transnational campaigns around the topic of violence against women. The campaign, which aimed to prevent harmful traditional practices against women and girls, has

---

110 Merry 2006, p 12. When culture does appear in discussions about European or North American countries, it refers to the ways of life of immigrant communities and/or racial minorities. Volpp, 2000, p 90: "Under this scheme white people are individual actors, people of colour are members of groups." See also below, where we discuss the tendency in the current nationalists discourses in the West where all immigrants that adhere to Islam are portrayed by some politicians and opinion leaders as backward, traditionalist people that should preferably return to their home countries.

111 Merry 2006, p 10–11.

112 Volpp 2001, p 1192.

113 UN Special Rapporteur on VAW; 'Intersections between culture and violence against women', 17 January 2007, UN Doc. A/HRC/4/34, para. 46 ff. See also Merry 2006, Chapter 3.

helped to identify types of violence against women which were formerly not recognised, and has mobilised considerable international and local constituencies for their eradication. It focussed on several reproductive health issues, in particular on female genital mutilation.[114] However, it "(...) unfortunately reinforced the notion that metropolitan centres of the West contain no tradition or culture harmful to women, and that the violence which does exist is idiosyncratic and individualised rather than culturally condoned."[115] The UN Special Rapporteur on Violence Against Women initially retained that divide, but changed this in her 2002 annual report,[116] in which she made it unambiguously clear that domestic violence is a world wide phenomenon, rooted in culture everywhere on the globe. The Special Rapporteur thus contributed to a paradigm shift in the way cultures are addressed and considered within a human rights framework.[117]

Arguing for the abolishment of cultural practices

From a discourse in which culture is seen as something (static) that exists 'out there' and that functions as an obstacle to the full implementation of women's human rights, it is a small step to calling for the abolition, eradication or extinction of such culture, or of particular practices within that culture. Feminists who campaigned for the implementation of women's human rights often have tended to demand the complete abolition of certain religious or traditional practices, mainly through demanding State action to prohibit or penalise such traditions or customs, and to ask for severe punishment when the legal prohibition is violated. When speaking about cultural change these advocates of women's human rights seemed to mean to abolish the oppressive culture altogether.[118] But by doing so, the role of violator of women's human rights was attributed to culture, not to individuals or institutions that have a stake in maintaining the oppressive practices and beliefs that are part of this culture.[119] By presenting a culture as monolithic and static, opportunities to use openings that are present within each culture are rejected, and in fact the *status*

114 Packer 2002, p 4.

115 Winter et al 2002, p 72–94.

116 UN Special Rapporteur on VAW, 'Cultural practices in the family that are violent against women'; 31 January 2002, UN Doc. E/CN.4/2002/83.

117 See also UN Special Rapporteur on VAW, '15 Years of the United Nations Special Rapporteur on Violence Against Women, Its Causes and Consequences (1994–2009), a Critical Review'; 27 May 2009, UN Doc. A/HRC/11/6/Add.5. See also the Rapporteur's 2007 Report, mentioned above.

118 A strong abolitionist stance may be found in Moller Okin 1987.

119 This is sometimes called 'enculturing' women's inequality', that is: seeing the causes thereof solely in terms of culture, not in terms of e.g. economic oppression and exploitation (e.g. by the West or by capitalist companies), or of internal and external military conflicts. See e.g. Merry 2003 Polar. See also above, where we discuss who have a vested interest in sustaining certain oppressive cultural practices.

quo as to who defines and represents what the particular culture entails is confirmed. It is either male leadership of these cultures, or advocates for women's human rights; in any case it hardly ever is women who actually (still) live within these cultures.[120] They are seen as mere victims of their own culture.

The process or orientalising culture and the call for their abolition (preferably through severe criminal punishment, or even expulsion of the perpetrators of human rights violations from the country) is also taking place at the national level in many of today's Western societies. The 'other' culture, in that instance, is the culture of certain immigrant communities, which are declared to be 'traditional', ' pre-modern', 'backward', or even 'evil' or 'bad'.[121] Such arguments are in fact directed against large Muslim immigrant communities. Susanne Baer rightfully points out that in many political discussions this process takes the form of 'othering sex inequality'.[122] That means: other than national, local, i.e. Western cultures are seen as backward, pre-modern, repressive, or what-not, because they supposedly do not recognise or subscribe to the principle of sex equality and adhere to practices and beliefs in which women are not seen as equals to men.

What happens in such (highly politicised) discourses is that the problem of women's inequality is only attached to these other (i.e. not local, not dominant) alien or immigrant cultures, and that it is made to appear as if the majority or the *original* culture does not have any problems with women's inequality or gender discrimination. "By othering sex inequality, a majority pretends to finally become feminist, but does so in a watered down version of feminism, and instead envisages in, ultimately, racist politics."[123] This strategy "uses religion or culture as a stigma to shield a majority from critique and change."[124] Often advocates for women's human rights in that process design an essentialist, monolithic and

120 Even if the advocates for women's human rights originally come from the particular country or cultural group, they often are estranged from this group when they demand women's full equality in international (legal) forums. Merry (2006) gives many examples of this (sad) process.

121 Often, in such discourses, it is argued that such 'backward' cultures are not (yet) familiar with human rights norms, or – the other way around – that human rights are inherent in the Western / modern tradition, ergo are at odds with traditionalists cultures. See also para. 2.1, where we describe how the debate about the coming into being of human rights is captured by some who see this development as an automatic outcome of the history of European civilisation.

122 Baer 2010, p 61: "*Othering* is a strategy to locate a problem elsewhere and to remain categorically clean, untouched; and *orientalising* is othering in a particular mode, establishing the occident as the unlabelled standard and the orient as different, dark, elsewhere, the problem."

123 Baer 2010, p 62. By a watered down version of feminism, she means a version that takes a symmetrical or formal version of sex-equality as its main goal, thereby ignoring the more radical feminist claim of asymmetrical or substantive equality. (See para. 2.2).

124 Ibid, p 58.

static picture of such other or alien cultures (and indirectly also of their 'own' culture). It should be noted that claims that certain practices (e.g. wife beating) are in a definite way prescribed by a certain religion (say Islam) are most often not made by religious leaders, but by Western (right wing) politicians or opinion leaders, who next declare that this religion is 'backward' or even 'evil' and should not be allowed to undermine the enlightened Western (Christian/Judaeo) value system.[125] Also, some feminist women who have transgressed the border between their culture of origin and the dominant Western culture where they have come to live in, describe their original culture in essentialist terms.[126]

In most instances, however, the persons who voice these views are not women who belong to that particular minority culture, but members of the dominant Western societies, who present certain women-oppressive practices and beliefs that stem from an immigrant culture as unique, unchangeable or even as definitely prescribed by the holy texts of certain religions. Public opinion leaders and political leaders subsequently present certain manifestations of such cultures as being dangerous or oppressive for *all* women, not only for those who are part of a particular minority culture. For example, they state that Islamic headscarves signal the inferiority and subordination of *all* women and should therefore be banned from all public places in any secular State.[127]

Cultural relativism

Remarkably so, the opposite stance (i.e. opposite to orientalising culture and to pleading for the abolition or punishing of certain 'bad' cultures), is also based on essentialist notions of culture and gender. This opposite stance is often called 'multiculturalism' or 'cultural relativism'.[128]

In the course of the twentieth century, cultural relativism was developed in anthropological literature as a response to earlier held views within that academic discipline that human nature evolves from 'primitive' to 'modern'.[129] Cultural

125 See e.g. Saharso 2002 and Holtmaat 2002(b). In The Netherlands, the feminist / politician Ayaan Hirshi Ali (see: www.ayaanhirsiali.web-log.nl/ayaanhirsiali/english/index.html; last accessed on July 20, 2010) is a rare exception to the fact that mostly males voice these concerns. However, Hirshi Ali in the same vein portrays the Islamic faith in an essentialist way.

126 See the example of Hirshi Ali, discussed above.

127 For a critical discussion of the headscarf discussion in France and the ethnocentricity of many French feminists, see Delphy 2009.

128 See the Volume of very influential papers edited by Amy Goodman 1994. In the remainder of this paragraph we only speak of cultural relativism.

129 NB: in the previous section we have discussed that such views still persist in the 'global – local' divide in which culture is orientalised, which divide is very often constructed in discourses about the difficulties surrounding implementation of global and universal human rights standards in local communities. See Merry 2003 Polar.

relativism was introduced to combat the notions that were used to rank Western societies highest and saw Western values as standards for a universal model for the evolution of all human societies. Under that banner the 'civilising' mission of Western colonialism enforced its own rule upon the population of the colonies, who were conveniently portrayed as 'barbarian', 'uncivilised' or (more neutrally) as 'Others'.

Cultural relativism, according to its purest proponents, acknowledges the *absolute equal validity and value* of diverse patterns of life and value systems, and stresses the need for tolerance of all other cultures, though they may to a great extend differ from one's own.[130] By placing all possible cultures on an equal level, it regards any given culture as a homogenous, monolithic entity that deserves equal respect and concern. It thus holds an essentialist view on culture. In order to be able to determine the fixed and static content and scope of a particular culture anthropologists have embraced dominant expressions thereof, as they were predominantly voiced by male leadership. This is highly problematic where women's perceptions and experiences were not incorporated in such representations.[131] As is the case with all other essentialist perspectives on culture, this way of portraying traditions, religious prescriptions and customs leaves no room for cultural change, including a change of gender relations. Furthermore, the danger of cultural relativism is that it undermines the ability to condemn oppressive practices that are sanctioned or sustained by a particular culture.[132] If *every* culture is valuable in itself and can only be judged by its own *internal* norms, the transnational or global culture of human rights ranks equal with all other local cultures, however contrary to the central human rights value of equal dignity and worth of *all* human beings these latter cultures might be.

By way of conclusion of this paragraph, we turn back to Yakin Ertürk's illuminating Report on the intersections between culture and violence against women. The UN Special Rapporteur neatly summarises why cultural essentialism is a real and eminent danger for women:

> "This report has argued that cultural essentialism, in its orientalist as well as occidentalist variations, are based on several myths that need to be challenged if we are to move forward in the international human rights agenda in general and the elimination of violence against women in particular. These are: (i) depicting culture as immutable and static; (ii) culture as homogenous; and (iii) culture as apolitical and

130 An-Na'im 1990, p 339–343.

131 The debate on these issues is fierce and has aroused a host of publications. See for a still influential Volume of papers Gutman 1994.

132 See the Government Response 24.03.2009 to Advice of Advisory Council on International Affairs 'Universality of Human Rights. Principles, Practice and Prospects' (November 2008). For more on this see Narayan 1998 p 100–104.

detached from the material foundation of life. Such myths privilege dominant representations of culture while denying space for alternative voices; they cloud over the material basis of life that underpins cultural claims, thus overlooking the political and economic conditions that sustain the violation of women's rights."[133]

3.4 A SPECIAL PLACE FOR RELIGION WITHIN CULTURE?

In this book we have subsumed religion under a broad concept of culture.[134] Religion or belief[135] is central to the daily lives of millions of people around the globe. Religion has often been understood in a variety of ways in different places and times but definitions usually include some transcendental belief in or service to the divine.[136] Religion enhances a creative side in human beings as basically it is able to provide a reference system, an ultimate meaning of life, or a founding truth. However, this positive, resourceful side of religion is inextricably linked to its more restrictive thus negative aspects. One major problem is, that it may become difficult for believers to tolerate other ideologies that offer contrasting claims to truth or prescribe other ways of inter-human behaviour.[137] Religion, in that way, may become a source for intolerance and even for violent conflicts about the ultimate ethical (behavioural) norms that govern human social and personal life.

Organised religions (whether seen as social movements with a membership structure or as dynamic cultural traditions) usually have some form of force and regulation imposed on their members or adherents. Personal convictions are channelled into some kind of official dogma, articulated in confessions, instructed in learning processes, transmitted in special forms of initiation and strengthened by sanctions for its trespassers. Religious leaders (almost always exclusively men) possess the authority and responsibility for the transmission of

---

133 Report of the UN Special Rapporteur on VAW, 'Intersections between culture and violence against women'; 17 January 2007, UN Doc. A/HRC/4/34, para. 70.

134 We realise that this may have the (risky) effect that freedom of religion is seen as a right of a group, like is the case with culture, not as the right of an individual. See Baer 2010, p 59. Baer calls this 'enculturalizing religion' and warns against the risk of 'groupism', i.e. constructing religious rights as rights of the religious group, instead of as individual (freedom) rights. See also para. 2.5. With the inclusion of religion within the wider concept of culture, we want to debunk religion from the special moral authority that often surrounds it, and want to avoid what Baer also signals, that religion gets special status, i.e. that religious people / organisations are allowed to discriminate, while other people / organisations are prohibited to do so. See Baer 2010, p 68.

135 As guaranteed in inter alia Article 18 UDHR – further only 'religion'.

136 Weller 2007, p 148.

137 Míguez 2000, p 142.

the religious tradition.[138] Especially the monotheistic scriptural religions have become an institutionalised aspect of culture, with customs codified into binding source books and bureaucratic institutions that are focal points for economic and political power within the society. These characteristics render religion less amenable to adaptive pressures from the outside, including from the international human rights community. Change must therefore be wrought from within.[139]

Religious beliefs in most parts of the world reinforce traditional patriarchal (or hierarchical) relations between the sexes. Traditional concepts of male superiority have combined with religious notions of female inferiority and incapacity. Or, with female 'sanctity' – especially related to motherhood, symbolised in the Christian Holy Mother Mary – which deserves special protection. Moreover, religions often reinforce notions of fatalism or spiritualism, telling their adherents that human relations as they are, are a mere expression of the will of God. Their deep-rooted values, norms and practices are highly influential in daily life with its social and cultural customs, and as such religious and cultural beliefs and practices have become indistinguishable.

In this book, we have described culture – including religion – as a human construction, and thereby as something that is subject to continuous change. A government that is party to CEDAW is obliged to modify certain cultural practices and beliefs when aspects of it obstruct the full realisation of the human rights of women. We realise that this stance is secular and is highly contested by those people who believe that there exists a natural order between the sexes, and even more so by those who believe that this order is constructed or ordained by a deity and is laid down in a holy text.[140] Still, the latter position does leave room for the view that religion is humanly constructed because one can make a distinction between religion as a *spiritual experience* and as a set of *rules and practices*.[141] The first might originate from the relationship with the Divine and therefore be unchangeable by men; the second being humanly constructed and subject to change. The main argument for this stance is that it is always (some)

---

138 Houtepen 2000, p 45.

139 Raday 2003, p 667–668.

140 We do not have the space to dig deeply into the debate about (State) secularism and religion. For that issue we refer to the extensive (often legal / constitutional) literature. An example of a project that tries to translate this literature to a more practical level (in the context of development co-operation) are the series of 'Pluralism Working Papers' which were issued in 2009 by the Promoting Pluralism Programme of HIVOS and The University for Humanistics in the Netherlands, the Centre for Religion and Cross-cultural Studies in Indonesia, the Centre for study of Culture and Society in India, and the Cross Cultural Foundation in Uganda. The Papers may be ordered from HIVOS: www.hivos.net.

141 We will return to this argument in para. 4.3, where we discuss the possibilities to support religious women in their struggle for internal reform. At that place, we will argue that this stance has problematic aspects.

human beings who have 'captured' or 'received' the natural or religious order and have put it into words, rules and practices. "Key to this notion of religion as mutable, rather than as a natural, unchanging essence, is the observation that while the subject matter of religion is spiritual and textual, it is human beings who interpret religion and make it meaningful for their time."[142]

Another often heard argument against the inclusion of religion in the wider concept of culture is that religion receives special protection by international human rights law and by national constitutional law. It is said that religion has higher standing as a result of the *expressis verbis* right to freedom of religion in most international human right treaties and national constitutions. However, it must be remembered that this right concerns the individual freedom of religion or belief and not a right of religion as such. It thus relates to the freedom of the individual to choose his or her own religion, to attend religious ceremonies and to live according to the accepted religious norms. And, as we have discussed in paragraph 2.5, one may not manifest one's religion unlimited and use it as justification for any kind of discrimination against women. It is important to realise that those people who claim this internationally guaranteed religious freedom (including the tradition to subjugate women to male power), while at the same time rejecting the authority of international legal norms that guarantee women's equality, thereby use a double standard. They reject the validity of secular law relating to women's equality, while at the same time relying on such secular law when it concerns their religious freedom.

With these last remarks, we have already embarked upon the undertaking of finding strategies to countervail the argument that culture does not allow the recognition and implementation of women's human rights. The next (and final) Chapter explores such strategies in more detail.

142 Sunder 2003, p 1423.

CHAPTER 4

FROM A FIRM DEADLOCK TO A FRUITFUL DIALOGUE

"Transformation works both ways, or not at all."[1]

"If discrimination is not fully exposed, it cannot be effectively opposed."[2]

This final Chapter discusses strategies that may be used to move from a deadlock to a dialogue about women's human rights and culture. We bring together insights that can be derived from the analysis of both key elements of our central question: women's human rights (Chapter 2) and culture and gender (Chapter 3), and from examples of good practices which we have derived from interviews with a number of resource persons who have a lot of practical experiences with the implementation of human rights 'on the ground'. In doing so, we discuss three different levels of strategic considerations. First, we look into the question why a dialogue is necessary and where the boundaries of such a dialogue lie.[3] Secondly, we describe some possible structural barriers to accepting women's human rights. Finally, we discuss what might be done to overcome a wide variety of causes and manifestations of resistance against cultural change.

At the very core of all these arguments and strategies is our conviction that the biggest obstacle to change is the tendency to essentialise both the notions of women's human rights and culture, leading any discussion about this issue into a firm deadlock. Change, therefore, starts with de-essentialising both notions and seeing them as sites for struggles over meaning and practices. In that respect, it is extremely important to reveal that culture is not as static and monolithic as it is often presented by cultural essentialists. But it is equally important to accept that human rights of women are subject to a continuous (progressive) dynamic

1 Prof. Myra Marx Ferree, Professor of Sociology, University of Wisconsin, Madison. Quoted from her key note speech at the Colloquium at the occasion of the farewell of Prof. Joyce Outshoorn, Leiden University 27 November 2009.

2 Katarina Tomaševski; quote derived from www.right-to-education.org/node/711 (accessed on 10 December 2009).

3 In Chapter 1 we have explained that of course such a dialogue is not solving all problems and that sometimes other means (like e.g. diplomatic pressure) are indicated.

interpretation, which takes context and time into account. Such an open-minded approach, we hope, will create possibilities to making some small first steps on the road to real progress as regards the elimination of all forms of discrimination against women.

PARTNERS IN THE DIALOGUE ABOUT WOMEN'S HUMAN RIGHTS AND CULTURE

When it is the aim to engage into a dialogue about women's human rights and culture it is important to establish who are the main discussion partners in this respect. A process of changing cultural practices and patterns of conduct that stand in the way of the full realisation of women's human rights can be envisaged through institutional changes, cultural changes and changes in individual capacities of women.[4] Various actors may contribute as 'change agents' in this respect. Close co-operation with all of these actors is necessary in the face of political and cultural resistance against the implementation of women's human rights.

For this reason, we describe dialogue strategies that can be employed in discussions with at least three different kinds of change-agents. First, there are national governments of States parties to human rights covenants, who are obliged to implement the internationally agreed standards as regards women's human rights. Governments of other States, international institutions, international and domestic non-governmental organisations (further: NGOs), and domestic social groups can each seek to influence a national governments' legislation and policies through enhancing a dialogue with government officials and politicians about women's human rights and culture. Secondly, male and female members of cultural (religious and traditional) communities may take part in community and cross-cultural dialogue programmes in order to build ownership of the agenda of human dignity, equality and rights.[5] Thirdly, individuals, such as women, religious leaders and community leaders may increase their knowledge, skills and self-confidence, and in that way they may contribute to enhancing cultural change. Any educational or training program

---

4 See Dutch policy paper 'Resultaten in Ontwikkeling. Rapportage 2007–2009' (Results in Development. Report 2007–2008), submitted to Parliament on 19 May 2009, TK 31 250 no. 59, appendix, p 72.

5 Cross-cultural programmes involve people from different cultures, often within the country itself. As is discussed in Chapter 3, it is important to make people who adhere to static, essentialist conceptions of culture and gender aware of the fact that there exists a diversity of cultural practices and believes; participation in cross-cultural programmes may enhance this awareness.

may contribute to this process of cultural change, especially when such programmes include education and training about women's human rights.

In interactions with each of these discussion partners or change agents, it is essential that existing local customs and traditions are respected:

> "Promotion of human rights does not mean that cultural diversity has to be sacrificed, but rather that within that diversity space to respect human rights is created. In this regard it is wise to express the human rights discourse as much as possible by means of local concepts, so as to take away the feeling that foreign cultural elements are being imposed. However, according to the Dutch Government the space for this translation is delineated by what is permitted in international treaties. The boundary should be clear."[6]

In this Chapter, both respect for cultural diversity and the boundaries to the acceptance thereof will be discussed. A final preliminary remark: each dialogue takes place in a particular cultural context, which varies from country to country and from region to region. For any discussion to be fruitful, good knowledge of this context is crucial, including knowledge about how gender relations are structured and sustained in a particular society. In this book there is no place to discuss such specificities in any detail.

4.1 THE NECESSITY AND THE BOUNDARIES OF A DIALOGUE

THE NECESSITY OF A DIALOGUE

Many academic commentators acknowledge that the only way out of a deadlock between opposite and fixed positions about women's human rights and culture is to engage into an intercultural or cross-cultural dialogue.[7] For example, Celestine Nyamu states that the process of cross-cultural dialogue

> "... calls for the pursuit of a global consensus viewing the relationship between international human rights and local culture as 'a genuine reciprocal global collaborative effort.' This two-way sharing of perspectives draws on the cultures' respective internal discourses. Through cross-cultural dialogue, external actors can

---

6 Dutch Government Response 24.03.2009 to Advice of Advisory Council on International Affairs 'Universality of Human Rights. Principles, Practice and Prospects' (November 2008), DMH/MR 137/09, p 8 [Translation by the authors].

7 E.g. Shachar 2001, Engle 2008, Philips 2007, Nyamu 2000 and An Na'im 1990.

support and influence the internal discourse, but they must take care not to undermine internal discourse."[8]

When one has to choose between on the one hand forcing other cultures to eradicate or abolish traditional practices that are deemed to violate women's human rights (and thereby most likely generating even more resistance), and on the other hand the position of cultural relativism, in which moral or ethical values seem to have no weight anymore, the most effective and safe middle way seems to be to try to start understanding each other and speaking with each other. In the words of Celestine Nyamu: "The non-abolitionist approach, therefore, calls for a non-hegemonic human rights practice that incorporates the two simultaneous processes of internal discourse and cross-cultural dialogue, in order to find legitimacy for human rights principles within all cultures."[9] Engaging into such a dialogue is also seen as the only way to guarantee that women's voices are heard in the process of implementation of human rights standards.[10]

Instead of using the word dialogue, some commentators talk about 'world travelling'. This is a three-pronged approach, which calls upon women's human rights advocates 1) to see themselves in historical context, 2) to see themselves as the cultural 'other' might see them, and 3) to see the cultural other within her/his own cultural context.[11] The third prong, according to Celestine Nyamu, recognises the complexities of the life and circumstances of other people in their particular contexts. The approach cautions against arrogant and imperialistic attitudes of Western activists that presume that these other 'cultural' people in fact are exactly like themselves,[12] or that presume to know exactly what is good for 'women of culture'.

In its Concluding Observations, the CEDAW Committee often stresses the necessity of engaging into a dialogue with civil society about cultural changes that need to take place in order to put an end to discrimination against women. It "(...) urges the State party to intensify co-operation in this regard with civil society organisations, women's groups and community leaders, traditional and religious leaders, as well as teachers and the media."[13] And it urges the State party "(...) to undertake such efforts in co-ordination with a wide range of stakeholders, and involving all sectors of society, so as to facilitate social and

8 Nyamu 2000, p 394. At this place, she quotes An Na'im 1994, p 173.

9 Nyamu 2000, p 393.

10 Currently, this strategy is getting more and more political and scholarly attention in all areas of legal pluralism or multi-layered jurisdictions. See e.g. Filippo Fontanelli et al (eds) 2009.

11 Nyamu 2000, p 395, referring to the work of Gunning 1992. See also Otto 1997.

12 Nyamu 2000, p 395.

13 CO Nigeria, CEDAW/C/NGA/6 (2008) para. 323.

cultural change and the creation of an enabling environment that is supportive of gender equality."[14]

Although the Committee here refers to the *internal* dialogue within a State party, it is important to communicate this stance widely and refer to it whenever a State party is unwilling to implement the Convention at this point.

UNIVERSALITY OR RELATIVITY?

The concept of human rights in its very core, rests on the fundamental principle of equality, i.e. on the principle that human rights belong to *all* human beings, irrespective of any categorisation between them on the basis of such characteristics as nationality, sex, sexual orientation, race, religion, cultural or ethnic origin, disablement, wealth, education, et cetera. (See para. 2.1.) In the human rights discourse, this principle is also expressed as the principle of universality. However, by using that particular expression, one may also mean to say that the *content and scope* of human rights is the same and should be interpreted and implemented in exactly the same manner everywhere on the planet. Of course the two conceptions of universality are closely interrelated: if a particular human right is deemed to be applicable to all, it should also be applicable to all in the same manner.

However important this principle may be, in our view the second meaning of universality may never mean that human rights are seen as a kind of 'holy text', the content and meaning of which is determined once and for all, leading to a static and monolithic application of this text.[15] Such application would preclude a dynamic interpretation of existing human rights documents, and would make any dialogue about the development of human rights virtually impossible. Presenting human rights as 'absolute truths' about which no further discussion is possible, will certainly lead to a high level of frustration of all those people who feel that until now they have not had a chance to fully participate in their development. For women, this is certainly a big problem, since in large parts of

---

14 CO Nicaragua, CEDAW/C/NIC/CO/6 (2007) para. 12.

15 This would lead to essentialising human rights and to denying their historical and geographical context and the struggle over their meaning and scope, that takes place continuously, also in the Western world. See para. 2.1. See also Baer 2010, p 64, and Bielefeldt 2000 (p. 92), who states that "[W]hat is needed (...) is a critical defense of universal human rights in a way that gives room for different cultural and religious interpretations, and at the same time avoids the pitfalls of cultural essentialism." The latter author discusses to some extent that human rights doctrine may not be seen as a moral philosophy or a religion, because it does not offer us definite answers to existential questions about the meaning of life and death, and it does not provide us with rituals and symbols through which we can express our mutual respect and give meaning and structure to our social life. (Ibid, p 116).

the world women's concerns and ideas about human rights have not been (fully) included in the process of adopting the existing human rights documents, including CEDAW, and in the process of their implementation at national level.

A certain 'relativity' or 'openness' of the meaning and scope of human rights is therefore unavoidable and necessary for the purpose of their further development within the context of a true cross-cultural or intercultural dialogue about their interpretation and implementation, as well as in the interest of their further development to areas that until now have not been brought under their scope.[16]

Such openness does not mean that no boundaries as to what is acceptable or not acceptable behaviour are set (see also below). It does also not mean that all cultural expressions are seen as equally valuable, and that therefore no interference is possible, as is the stance of 'cultural relativists'. It does mean, however, that more space is made for cultural specific applications of human rights in diverse contexts all over the world. According to the Dutch Advisory Council on International Affairs, the principle of universality of human rights should go hand in hand with respect for cultural diversity.[17] Culture, it should not be forgotten, is extremely important for people's dignity and full development as human beings, and therefore, respect for cultural diversity should rank very high on the ladder of the most basic principles of human rights.

The two positions (universalism / relativism) are often constructed as completely oppositional, and thereby the discussion about the issue becomes highly polarised. There is an "imperative to express absolute, uncompromising positions on both sides'.[18] Creating a dichotomy between on the one hand universality of human rights and cultural relativism on the other hand also means that the reality of women's lives is being denied: "Human lives are constituted by interlocking communities – ranging from the world to our countries, and our local communities to our work, religion, family, nationality, language and ethnicity. The oppositional stance that views these complementary locations in juxtaposition to, rather than in tandem with, each other ignores the reality and context within which people exist in society."[19]

---

16 Compare the way in which the topic of Violence Against Women was brought under the scope of CEDAW in CEDAW GR 19. Otto 1997 understands universality of human rights as 'transformative', i.e. as a motor or vehicle for real transformations of relationships of power. According to her, universality should be "understood as dialogue, in the sense of struggle, rather than as a disciplinary civilizing mission of Europe." (at p 5).

17 Advice of Advisory Council on International Affairs 'Universality of Human Rights. Principles, Practice and Prospects' (November 2008) (Dutch only).

18 Otto 1997, p 3. In that way, a transformative understanding of human rights becomes impossible.

19 Hernàndez-Truyol 2002, p 146.

WOMEN'S HUMAN RIGHTS AS THE BOTTOM LINE

A dialogue between human rights advocates and cultural leaders and/or 'women of culture', can only be successful when both sides taking part realise that *talking with one another* does not mean *talking to the other* in terms of prescribing the other what to think or what to do. Having a dialogue also means that one understands (or at least wants to listen to) why the other participants find something 'fundamental' or 'sacred', and thereby something that cannot easily be negotiated or changed. However, it is equally important to know what for himself or herself are fundamental principles or rights that can not be 'talked away'. Talking *with* someone is also not the same as talking *along with* someone.[20]

From the position of advocates of women's human rights, this means that the bottom lines of a dialogue with the defenders of a particular harmful cultural practice must be clear from the outset. This bottom line is often drawn at the level of obligatory compliance to international human rights standards. Exemplary of this is the stance of the Dutch Ministry of Foreign Affairs: "However, as for the Dutch Government the space for this translation is delineated by what is permitted in international treaties. *The boundary should be clear.*"[21] [Italics added.] In other words: At the international legal level we have already firmly established the bottom line for the exchange of views in the dialogue about the position of women.

Although in principle we fully agree with this stance, demarcating this boundary in this way is not *the* simple solution to the perceived clash or incompatibility between women's human rights and culture. An important reason for this is that such firm language does not offer as much clarity and stronghold as one might hope and expect. For, although there are indeed international legal documents in which women's human rights are codified as positive law (most notably in CEDAW), it should always be remembered that – as is the case with all law – these legal norms are open to interpretation and evolution. The CEDAW Committee, for instance, time and again stresses that this Convention "is subject to continuous dynamic interpretation".[22] This means that the exact content and scope of the obligations under CEDAW are not determined once and for all with the adoption of the Convention by the UN General Assembly in 1979, but that these obligations may develop over time. Exemplary of this is the fact that, although the term 'violence against women' is mentioned nowhere in the Convention, there now is general agreement about the fact that this is indeed

20 "Talk with them, but don't talk their talk." Berger 2006, p 17.

21 Government Response 24.03.2009 to Advice of Advisory Council on International Affairs 'Universality of Human Rights. Principles, Practice and Prospects' (November 2008), DMH/MR 137/09, p 8 [Translation by the authors].

22 CEDAW GR 25, para. 3.

prohibited under CEDAW.[23] However, in this respect there is also a bottom line: the dynamic interpretation of CEDAW must be a *progressive* interpretation, in the sense of contributing to the achievement of the Convention's overall goals, i.e. to the improvement of the conditions of life and the empowerment of women. This is the reason why the Committee is unambiguous in its stance that women's human rights take priority over those expressions of culture or cultural practices that are harmful for women or deny women the full enjoyment of their human rights. (See para. 2.4.)

4.2 STRUCTURAL BARRIERS TO ACCEPTING WOMEN'S HUMAN RIGHTS

THE LIMITED EFFECTS OF SETTING THE BOUNDARY

With the principle of progressive dynamic interpretation in mind, internationally agreed women's human rights can indeed be seen and presented as boundaries that may not be transgressed and that set the bottom line for any dialogue about the position of women. States that have signed up to CEDAW have an *international obligation* to respect women's human rights as included in this Convention and can be held *accountable under international law* for any violation of these rights, even when these violations take place in the private sphere (between citizens). However, people who (openly) follow this line of argument must be aware that, in order to expect any real effect of using it, there has to be some degree of acceptance by all participants of the dialogue of the basic premises of women's human rights as a legal / normative system. These premises are situated on

1. the ethical / moral level, concerning the values underlying them; and on the
2. the level of international relations, relating to
   a. a limitation of the State's sovereign powers as to how the State may treat its own citizens / inhabitants;
   b. a positive obligation to implement human rights standards within the country; accepting responsibility for human rights violations by non-state actors.

Without acceptance of these premises by all parties in the dialogue, using the argument that according to international law States are obliged to respect women's human rights will hardly have any effect. *The other party will simply not agree with it.* And that means the end of the discussion, after which the State that

23 See CEDAW GR 12 and 19.

has used this argument in the first place needs to find ways of holding the other State accountable under international law for violations of women's human rights. But even when a State formally accepts these basic premises of the discussion, much depends on whether these legal arguments are presented in such a way that they are not perceived as a one way prescription of how to behave, or as yet another imposition of culture-alien norms and values by Western neo-colonisers. How this may be avoided is discussed in more detail in the second part of this Chapter. Before doing so, in the third part of this paragraph we analyse the above mentioned barriers in more detail.

BARRIERS TO ACCEPT THE NORMATIVE PREMISES OF HUMAN RIGHTS

Diplomats and civil servants, and all other human rights advocates who stand up for the implementation of women's human rights, should be aware of the historical/normative dimensions of them (see para. 2.1). Human rights are firmly linked to

1. basic values/norms underlying the construction of the democratic (constitutional) legal order;
2. the moral and ethical value orientation, in which the freedom/autonomy and equality and equal dignity of the individual human being is at the very centre.

Those who claim that their culture does not allow for the implementation of women's human rights often implicitly or explicitly resist against one or both of these basic assumptions. They instead hold that::

1. not everybody can participate in society or in public and political life, since some people's (read: women's) role lies at the home, not in conducting public affairs; and/or
2. the continuation of (institution of) the family / the cultural group / the traditional society is far more important than upholding the rights and freedoms of 'mere' individuals.[24]

The first argument is based on one of the most persistent and all pervasive gender stereotypes, which constructs an unbridgeable gap between private and public life.[25] It is very well known in The Netherlands, since it lies at the core of the

24 In that way, a 'clash' between liberal values and communitarian values is constructed. See Gutman 1994.

25 See e.g. Pateman 1988 and Amaya-Castro 2010.

so-called 'SGP issue', concerning a fundamentalist Christian political party that denies women the right to equal political participation claiming that this is what the bible proscribes.[26] The long and fierce discussions in Dutch society and the many legal proceedings about this issue illustrate how difficult it is to judicially counteract this argument. The fact that several Dutch judges now have accepted that the international legal norm of Article 7 CEDAW indeed does not allow this argument, must be seen as a great victory. Dutch judges, in this respect, finally are prepared to set a boundary.[27]

The second argument relates to the difficult question of whether individual rights or group rights should prevail.[28] The 'right *to* culture' is something very different from the 'right *of* a culture'.[29] The first refers to the right of an individual to enjoy his/her culture – including religion – and to participate in it (see e.g. Articles 18 and 27 ICCPR), the second to the right of particular cultural groups to be treated equally as other cultural groups, or to be accepted and supported in the perseverance of their culture (see e.g. *UNESCO Convention on the Protection and Promotion of Cultural Expressions*). In international human rights law, the position is taken that the rights of individual human beings in principle prevail over group rights.[30] According to international legal standards, even when individuals who claim their human rights with such actions undermine the community (e.g. by claiming a right to exit, or to criticise certain cultural values that hold this community together), their individual rights must be upheld.[31] Human beings are an *end in themselves* and can never be used as a *means* to guarantee the survival of a cultural community or the preservation of a certain culture.

The perception of what it means to be a human being which underlies the concept of human rights, in which the individual male and female human being is seen as (in principle) capable of making informed and rational decisions about his/her own course of life, is alien to many cultures in which stereotyped (and

---

26 See Boerefijn 2010.

27 See in particular the judgement of the highest administrative court (Afdeling Bestuursrechtspraak Raad van State-ABRvS) of 5 December 2007, LJN: BB9493 and the judgement of the Supreme Court (Hoge Raad) of 9 April 2010, LJN: BK4549. These judgements may be downloaded from the internet site www.rechtspraak.nl, by using their LJN reference number. (Dutch only).

28 See also paras 2.5. and 3.4.

29 See Galenkamp 1993, who investigates the notion of collective (human) rights.

30 See e.g. Article 2 of the UNESCO Convention on the Protection and Promotion of Cultural Expressions (2005). See also para. 3.4, where it is discussed whether religious rights deserve special treatment in this respect.

31 This is not always accepted in national court proceedings. See e.g. the case of Ms Martinez and her daughter, claiming membership of an 'Indian tribe', while tribal membership rules excluded the daughter, dismissed by the US Supreme Court. SANTA CLARA PUEBLO v. MARTINEZ, 436 U.S. 49 (1978). For more about this issue, see Charles Taylor in his contribution to Gutman 1994.

different) capacities and roles of men and women are seen as natural, predestined or as God-given. In this perspective, any change in the relations between the sexes will lead people away from this natural or religious order and will bring unhappiness or even disaster upon the cultural community.

A possible answer to this anxiety could be to (cautiously) show people that human beings in different times around the world have adopted different traditions or beliefs, but that nevertheless they have not perished; and that some features of their own culture have indeed actually changed over time. Everyone knows the stories of elderly people about how different things were when they were young. Everyone has experienced in his/her own lifetime that other patterns of behaviour between men and women have evolved. Very often, people sentimentalise the past when things were deemed to be better or more in accordance with *natural* human relations. It is important to discuss examples (preferably from the participants to the dialogue themselves) of how bad some things were in the past and of what important improvements cultural change has brought. As was said in the introduction to this Chapter, it is extremely important to reveal that culture is not as static and monolithic as it is presented by cultural essentialists. This means that in any situation where culture is presented in such a way, it is necessary to break open this monolithic and static picture. Broad and generalised statements about a particular culture can be counteracted with evidence of alternative practices and of gradual social and cultural change. Evidence of historical and situational variations in cultural expressions is plentiful in local practices and may serve as powerful counter arguments to rigid or absolutist claims about 'the true character' of a culture.[32] Alternative cultural expressions may not necessarily be verbalised, but may be evident in practices of resistance. They may be gathered through empirical fieldwork and presented to official and semi-official forums that play a key role in the definition and official articulation of cultural norms, such as, for example, by religious leaders, by official advisory councils or in judicial proceedings.[33] Supporting local research initiatives in this area could therefore be one of the general strategies to enhance more openness for cultural change.

A second strategy to arrive at more acceptance of the human rights moral value orientation is to explore and reveal the actual values of the particular community that are embedded in or are underlying in their culture. Often, these cultural practices signify a great deal of respect for human dignity and for the unique characteristics and contributions of the individual members of the community. Women, for example, are often celebrated and honoured for their reproductive capacities and for their caring attitudes. However gender stereotyped such values

32 Nyamu 2000, p 413.

33 Nyamu 2000, p 413/4; An-Na'im 1990, p 357.

may be (since they are ascribed exclusively to women), they show that the notions of human dignity and respect for human life are not unfamiliar within such cultures. (See also para. 4.3, where we discuss the necessity of finding a common moral language.)

The principle of *human dignity* means that individual human beings have value as *ends in themselves*, and may not be used as a *means* to achieve some community goals. Bridging the gap between human rights and culture also means showing that the value orientation of human rights does not mean that in this moral and ethical value orientation human beings are ultimately being seen as completely *separate* or *isolated* from their family and their cultural community, and having no responsibilities towards their community. Many well established human rights fully acknowledge the fact that human beings cannot flourish and exist without family, religion, language, culture, or tradition. Human Rights Conventions do in fact *recognise* and *support* the right to family life, the right to religion, and the right to language, culture and tradition. They recognise and guarantee that individual human beings can only fully grow and develop themselves in these cultural contexts. Like the Universal Declaration stresses in Article 1: "All human beings are born free and equal in dignity and rights. They are endowed with reason and conscience *and should act towards one another in a spirit of brotherhood.*" [Italics added.] Human rights do in fact entail the *individual's responsibilities* towards human society. Therefore, it is important to counteract false representations of human rights as always and automatically leading to egocentric, individualistic or irresponsible behaviour of human beings that will always and automatically undermine the cultural community.

ACCEPTING INTERFERENCE WITH DOMESTIC AFFAIRS

As for the level of international relations, we presume that diplomats and other civil servants already use their 'tool kits' with international legal arguments and political and economic pressure in favour of norm-conformity in the area of human rights. A national government with whom they engage into a discussion about women's human rights may foster legislative amendments, policies and programmes that rule out gender discrimination within its legal and institutional framework and contribute to a heightened awareness and acceptance of equality of women and men. Mechanisms such as political pressure, economic or cultural coercion, persuasion or acculturation (or a combination of them) can lead to the adoption of women's human rights documents and new national legislation or policies, and can support effective implementation of these standards.[34] Most States that are a member of the United Nations have adopted CEDAW and other

34 Avdeyeva 2007, p 877–900.

relevant human right treaties. On that basis, they are obliged under international law to implement the principle of women's equality and dignity.[35] This fact can be used in a strategy to convince these States that a real and effective implementation of the non-discrimination standards in this Convention is obligatory. Diplomats and other representatives of a government who want to advocate for women's human rights, may use this argumentation whenever appropriate. However, such a strategy may in fact appear not to be effective. In order to understand why this is so, it is important to recognise that the topic of changing prevailing unequal gender relations touches upon issues that many States parties consider to be part of their national identity, and to be belonging to their absolute sovereignty.

From research into the mechanisms of international relations, it appears that "States apparently are more willing to negotiate, in other words seem less attached to their sovereignty, when material issues are at stake, as opposed to normative questions."[36] The conclusion from this research is that "(...) all States shared their reluctance to part with social and cultural practices", and that "(...) social values, more so than economic or military power, are the strongest aspects of global civil society's challenges to autonomy and legitimacy."[37] This even more so, when the construction of fixed gender identities and gender roles lies at the basis of the national identity of a country, which is the case with many post-colonial and traditionalist countries that have strong links with certain religious beliefs or religious institutions. (See para. 3.3.) This means that advocates of women's human rights who want to use international pressure and international legal instruments, should realise that without fundamental changes at the level of a State party's local normative system of values and beliefs not much may be achieved. Therefore, perhaps the attention should first be directed to finding adequate instruments for enhancing change at that level.

THE LEGAL AND CULTURAL LEGITIMISATION TO MODIFY CULTURE AND UNEQUAL GENDER RELATIONS

From the very beginning, the CEDAW Committee has acknowledged that a change of culture requires the strong political will of a State party to effectively do so: "[M]embers emphasised that attitudes and behaviour could be changed if

35 Equality and human dignity are the two main fundamental principles underlying all human rights conventions. State's who have signed up to these Conventions are obliged to 'respect, protect, fulfil and promote' these rights. See para. 2.1.

36 See Van den Brink 2008, p 73, who discusses research done by Hochstetler, Clark & Friedman 2000.

37 Ibid, p 75, quoting Hochstetler, Clark & Friedman 2000, p 611–612.

there was political will and broad support."[38] Even if a State is willing to bow its head under international pressure or is voluntarily willing to accept international human rights norms, it may be very difficult for it to effectively implement these norms in the internal legal order – also at the horizontal level (i.e. between private parties or citizens among themselves). This is particularly so when such international norms require a change of well established patterns of conduct which are based on tradition, religion, custom or culture of many of its inhabitants. This most certainly is the case with the norm of Article 5 CEDAW, on the basis of which States parties have *to modify the social and cultural patterns of conduct of men and women*, and to educate their citizens about *a proper understanding of maternity as a social function and the common responsibility of men and women*. In order to be able to implement these norms, it is necessary that the State is *legally* and *culturally* legitimised to enforce or even promote such change.[39] The necessary legal legitimisation for the implementation of Article 5 CEDAW can be found in the fact that the State has ratified this Convention.[40] After ratification of a Human Rights Convention, a government – be it monistic or dualistic in respect of the effects of international law on its own legal system – may simply argue (for example in its Parliament, answering political opposition) that it is obliged to implement the norms that are included in it. However, cultural legitimisation, especially when it concerns equality between men and women, is far more difficult to find / achieve because it requires modifying or overcoming very deeply rooted gender stereotypes and fixed parental gender roles, as we have discussed in Chapter 3.

The effectiveness of programs to modify gender stereotypes and fixed parental gender roles will most probably be very limited if the State party internally lacks cultural legitimisation to do so, i.e. if there is no connection with norms and values that (also) exist in its society, in particular with norms and values that women themselves consider to be of crucial importance for their lives and for the realisation of their human rights. States will certainly have difficulty finding this (internal) cultural legitimisation when there are important cultural majorities or even minorities that oppose to women's equality.[41] In such situations women's (equal) rights are often constructed as opposite to a nation's culture or to particular (minority or majority) religious rights. This makes implementation, even by governments who are highly committed to women's human rights, a very difficult issue. One of the strategies of advocates of women's human rights, could be to help the State party to enhance or broaden this necessary cultural

38 CO Ecuador, UN Doc.A/49/38, 13th Session (1994) para. 524.

39 See Packer, p 15 and Chapter VIII.

40 States parties are obliged to implement international norms in good faith, et cetera. See Cook 1994, p 229 ff. See also CO Portugal, CEDAW/C/PRT/CO/7 (2008) para. 29.

41 This issue is related to the topic of the necessary 'symbolic validation' of the human rights norms. See para. 3.2, where we discussed the work of Hernández-Truyol.

legitimisation. One of the routes to achieve this, is not only to stimulate a dialogue between the State and international actors (for instance the CEDAW Committee), but also to promote and enhance a dialogue between the State and the main internal stakeholders, i.e. religious leaders, community leaders and (women's) NGOs.[42]

4.3 POSSIBLE RESPONSES TO THE RESISTANCE AGAINST CULTURAL CHANGE

The causes and manifestations of resistance against cultural change are manifold. This reflects the fact that gender is constructed and reproduced on *all* levels in society, from the individual identity to institutional and structural features of society at large or even of the State itself. For that reason, the full realisation of women's human rights can only be envisaged through institutional changes, cultural changes and changes in individual capacities of women.[43] In Chapter 3, we discussed the central role that culture – and with it the gender relations that are embedded in it – plays in the construction of the identity of groups and nations and of individual men and women. We also discussed the fact that unequal gender relations lie at the basis of what is perceived of as *natural* family relations. There are many different stakeholders within a particular cultural community to maintain this status quo. Here we discuss how these stakeholders could be approached in the dialogue about women's human rights and culture.

RECOGNISING VESTED INTERESTS OF MEN AND SEEKING A WIN-WIN SITUATION

In Chapter 2 we concluded that human rights are never a quiet possession. There is always a (political) power struggle involved, when people claim that their human rights should be respected. In the case of the human rights of women, the struggle is mainly about the roles and tasks of men and women, in which women most often are confined to those areas of life where there is no autonomy or independence for them. Men, on the other hand are in a position of power, not only in public affairs but also at home, and profit highly from the subordinated position of women. A thorough analysis of who is going to gain and who is going to lose when human rights of women are being effectively implemented is a necessary precondition for a real discussion about this issue with stakeholders in

42 See the recommendations, made by the CEDAW Committee, as cited above.

43 See Dutch policy paper 'Resultaten in Ontwikkeling. Rapportage 2007–2009' (Results in Development. Report 2007–2008), submitted to Parliament on 19 May 2009, TK 31 250 no. 59, appendix, p 72.

a particular country that exhibits strong resistance to women's human rights. Female stakeholders often still have to be convinced that there is something to gain from claiming their human rights; male stakeholders are often anxious that they may need to give up their privileged position.

However, presenting this issue as a clash or a struggle between the interests of men and women is not always the best possible strategy. On the contrary, people tend to avoid struggles and clashes, because these disrupt their lives and they don't know in advance what the outcome may be. They might win, but it is also conceivable that they will end up empty handed. Therefore, it is a challenge to somehow make clear that *everyone* may gain from implementing women's human rights, i.e. that both women and men are able to win something from them. Research done by psychologists in the area of implementation of anti-discrimination legislation has shown that people are far more willing to change their deeply rooted convictions and behaviours when they are convinced that there is something for them to gain from such change, than when they are just simply compelled to oblige to legal norms.[44]

Lately more attention is being given to raising awareness among men. Some programmes may be somewhat superficial and only to be window dressing. Informants told us that in some initiatives from men only, with a majority of the staff being male, the debates tend to go in strange directions. The amount of international funding that such programmes receive diminishes the funding for women's organisations. It may be more appropriate to hire qualified male staff within women's organisations and then develop men's awareness programmes within that particular context.

RECOGNISING WOMEN'S INTERESTS AT STAKE AND SEEKING A SAFE ENVIRONMENT FOR CHANGE

Often people who become familiar with severe violations of women's human rights do not take action against them, using the argument that the women involved agree with the practice, or even are involved in exercising this practice themselves. It seems clear that a genuine choice to accept certain cultural practices or religious norms should be accepted as valid, even if this disadvantages the acceptor. This liberty to choose is an essential part of the freedom of culture and religion and of the right to autonomy of each individual. (See Chapter 2.)

---

44 Prof. Naomi Ellemers, oral presentation at a research colloquium of the interdisciplinary working group on 'processes of in- and exclusion', Leiden University 14 October 2009.

However, recognition of individual women's consent to patriarchal relations and the concomitant disadvantages and harm for women, is problematic. Consent cannot be assumed from silence, since subjection to patriarchal authority inherently reduces the capacity for public dissent. Sometimes, in-egalitarian norms are so oppressive that, from the outset, they undermine the capacity of members of the oppressed group to exercise an autonomous choice to dissent. These oppressive practices can properly be recognised as hideous and women's consent will not validate them and thus should not be recognised.[45]

Women may also not be in the position to freely choose another way of life because they lack an understanding of themselves as citizens or subjects of law who have rights that may be violated.[46] They have long been habituated to the complete absence of basic human goods and rights or have been told that such goods and rights are not for them but only for men. Thus lifelong socialisation and the absence of information make individuals unable to change their preferences and desires to that other than what they perceive as 'natural' (i.e. cultural) relations between the sexes. According to Martha Nussbaum such adapted preferences are not appropriate indicators of whether women would do or do not want to change their lot. What thus counts as a political goal is that governments should see to it that women are enabled to exercise their human rights or, in Nussbaum's terminology, to enjoy and employ their central human capabilities.[47]

Women sometimes return to more traditional lives after having lived differently. For example, they may choose veiling after having lived unveiled. Or they may choose to live at home and take care of household and family, after having had employment outside the home. Often this is a change in their mode of functioning rather than in their level of political capability as citizens. Veiling or becoming a housewife does not mean that they wish to give up choices and opportunities in this area.[48] The bottom line is that women have a right to participate in all areas of life – including their culture, but at the same time they cannot be forced to participate or to stay within a culture that is oppressive to them. As the motto of Chapter 1 makes clear: there is indeed a right to fully enjoy one's culture, but this right does not mean that there is also a plight to stay within that culture or to leave it unchanged.[49]

---

45 Raday 2003, p 702.

46 Merry 2006.

47 Nussbaum 2000, p 87–88; An-Naím 1990, p 362 ff.

48 Nusbaum 2000, p 153.

49 Farida Shaheed, Independent United Nations Expert in the field of Cultural Rights in her first press statement, 23 November 2009.

RECOGNISING THE ROLE OF LOCAL LEADERSHIP

Previously (in para. 3.3), we have described that local (male) leadership, may have a vested interest in maintaining the status quo, as far as unequal gender relations are concerned. Any change in this respect may mean that women will get more opportunities to interfere with affairs that formerly were only decided by men. This includes the opportunity to co-determine content issues of a particular culture and the core values on which it is based. Male leadership, therefore, may fear stronger voices of women as a result of the implementation of women's human rights. This is particularly so in situations where males traditionally had the exclusive right to be a leader, a chief, priest or an elder in a religious or traditional community. Transformative female leadership programmes can facilitate women to be more visible in their communities and actively take part in community affairs and decision-making.[50]

Especially in religion, it is mostly men that have an exclusive say in interpreting religious texts, in conducting religious services or giving spiritual or religious advice.

While recognising that traditional religious belief systems have contributed to the subordination of women, traditional religious leaders and community leaders nevertheless may be extremely important in the process of change. This is because they can easily reach and have influence where the State cannot – at grassroots level, within the confines of the homes.[51] Often religious institutions and organisations actively participate in alleviating poverty and sometimes even move into the political arena to support this. Services are mostly provided at grassroots' level, such as education, health care and financial assistance. Therefore religious leaders and organisations are often more trusted than governmental authorities or international development co-operation organisations.[52] Seeking contact which such leaders and starting a dialogue with them, therefore might be a most important strategic instrument in the process of the implementation of women's human rights.

RECOGNISING THE STATE'S INTERESTS TO SUSTAIN OR MAINTAIN UNEQUAL GENDER RELATIONS

While dealing with governments that resist the implementation of women's human rights in the name of some essential features of their culture, government

50 E.g. Olubunmi Dipo-Salami, Emrakeb Assefa 2008.

51 Packer 2002, p 182–184.

52 Berger 2006, p 5.

officials of other States and others involved in the implementation of international human rights standards should be aware of the fact that these governments may have certain vested interests in presenting and preserving their culture in this way. As was described earlier (in para. 3.3) such governments may conceive and present their traditional and women-oppressive culture as essential for the nation's unique identity which can not be given up because this would 'make the country fall apart'.

Governments do not always openly use culture as an excuse not to accept or not to implement women's human rights. More often, this is done in a far more hidden or implicit way through the implementation of already existing (traditional or customary) social and legal structures with the help of State power. A country's social and cultural arrangements and power relations are reflected in its main institutions and in its laws and policies. This includes the institutional and legal construction of a country's gender relations. Celestine Nyamu argues that there is in fact a mutually reinforcing relationship between formal law and policy and cultural interpretations. "Formal law may operate to give a natural and immutable appearance to dominant articulations, and custom may be invoked to legitimise formal law. (...) A vague notion of culture provides a convenient scapegoat for government institutions and obscures the State's responsibility in redressing inequalities."[53]

A government may easily avoid addressing inequalities between women and men by claiming that it is powerless to alter existing social structures within the cultural sphere. This is even more the case when such structures have gained some guaranteed autonomy, or under the national Constitution are officially acknowledged as 'exemptions' to abide to the national (equality) laws of the country.[54] This, for example, may be the case with religious law or with customary law regarding family relations, inheritance or land law. It may be that traditional local communities have such immunities, or that churches have the right to adopt and implement their own laws or other normative systems, even when this leads to direct discrimination of 'others'. This happens all over the world, as Susanne Baer rightfully points out, where she discusses the fact that under European Union Directives regarding non-discrimination, churches have the right to discriminate, e.g. against homosexuals or against people from other religious communities. "Religions enjoy tremendous freedom to discriminate against all they define not to belong (...)."[55] Some post colonial Anglophone African countries have accommodated cultural and religious pluralism in the framework of their Constitutions. For example, the Kenyan Constitution

53 Nyamu 2000, 401.
54 Nyamu 2000, 400–406.
55 Baer 2010, p 64.

exempts from its anti-discrimination provision customary and religious laws in the areas of marriage, divorce, inheritance and other personal law matters. In addition, any customary law applicable to members of a particular race or tribe cannot be labelled discriminatory under this Constitution. Similar far reaching provisions are included in the Constitutions of Zimbabwe, Zambia and Ghana. These States thereby facilitate the preservation of discriminatory social (ethnical and gender) relations and, by excluding these areas from the normal political process of law making in the national Parliament, deny dissenting citizens a voice in shaping new social and cultural norms with respect to the (family law) relations between men and women.

An example of a country blaming its culture for bad behaviour against women[56], can be found in Kenya's Report to the Fourth UN Conference on Women (Beijing 1995). In this report Kenya stated that "(L)and title deeds were and are still issued to men and women without discrimination although due to cultural factors, men outnumber women". This was said to be the case because formal land title was registered in the name of the head of the household, who was presumed to be male. Even though no statutory requirement existed, Kenyan government officials justified this practice as a *reflection* of community culture. However, the cultural factors as referred to in the Kenyan report are as much a result of government action (legitimising the practice) as of the traditional social practice itself.[57]

Examples of African countries that did strike a balance between local diversity or legal pluralism and constitutional and human rights principles may be found as well. As such, Celestine Nyamu discusses the Constitutions of Uganda and South Africa, which did "surmount such pressure and [managed to] enact constitutional frameworks that do not grant immunity to the operation of personal laws. Their experiences demonstrate that it is possible to establish a constitutional framework that achieves a more fair balance between gender equality and the recognition of cultural and religious identity."[58]

SUPPORTING DIFFERENT STRATEGIES TO COMBAT DISCRIMINATION AGAINST WOMEN

In paragraph 2.2 it is explained that the CEDAW Convention in fact conceptualises women's equality in such a way that *formal*, *substantive* and

56 See Volpp 2000, who uses this phrase in the title of her article.
57 Nyamu 2000, p 402; see also Website Kenya Land Alliance www.kenyalandalliance.or.ke/issues/.
58 Nyamu 2000, p 410–411.

transformative equality are included. On this basis, the Convention calls for a holistic approach to combating discrimination against women. Not only should there be a firmly established individual right of women not to be discriminated against, there should also be supportive programmes and programmes aiming at structural change. This means that while working with governments that are unwilling or hesitant to implement women's human rights, or that shield behind culture, officials from other countries or from international humanitarian or human rights organisations should point out that all three strategies of combating discrimination against women should be followed. Sometimes it is strategically more effective to put the strategy of social support more on the foreground, sometimes the individual rights strategy may be more effective. However, neither of these two strategies, in the end, will lead to any real change as long as prevailing gender relations and the persistence of gender-based stereotypes are not addressed; i.e.: as long as a strategy of social and cultural change is not being followed as well.

Apart from the reasoning that CEDAW obliges States parties to follow this holistic approach, it could also be useful to point to this approach in order to countervail the argument that the concept of women's human rights is Western and that it is based on the premise (and strategy) of individuals claiming their individualistic rights. This objection does indeed have a basis. For a long time – in national and international law – the fundamental principles of equality and non-discrimination have been interpreted solely in a formal way. This formal approach to equality was deemed enough to give individuals the right to stand up against any form of unequal treatment or discrimination on the ground of (inter alia) sex. However adequate such an individual rights approach might be in some instances, it has proven to be absolutely insufficient for achieving the objective of the elimination of all forms of discrimination against women. The individual rights strategy pre-supposes that an individual woman who has been treated unequally or badly (e.g. has been subjected to sexual violence) is in the position to stand up against this injustice and to claim her rights in a court procedure. Nothing is less true.[59] Women are very much embedded in the 'close to home' social structures of the family and the cultural community. It is very hard for them to simply stand up and claim an *individual* right, even when serious harm is done to them. As has been shown in the works of many researchers who have criticised this individualistic model of human rights, a far more encompassing and community oriented approach to combating discrimination against women is necessary. In fact, CEDAW is not Western in

59 See e.g. the works of Merry, Packer and Nussbaum, discussed at several places in this book, who all argue (on the basis of their empirical observations) that most women can not and will not stand up for their individual rights in that way, because it will alienate them from their partner, family and/or community.

the sense that it only has an eye for this individualistic rights model. Therefore, it is important to point out to opponents of this model, that the Convention does not restrict itself to granting individual women the formal legal right to non-discrimination, but that it also calls for a strategy of social support (substantive quality) and of social and cultural change (transformative equality). The Convention in fact is as much oriented towards the rights and responsibilities of families and cultural communities, as it is oriented towards strengthening the rights of individual women.

INCLUDING WOMEN'S VOICES IN THE DIALOGUE

It is argued throughout this book that a great danger of the essentialist approach to culture is that the people who define – either from the inside or from the outside – what the essential characteristics of a particular culture are, are not the women who are subjugated to its oppressive and harmful practices. How, then, does one avoid speaking about culture without the involvement of women? In fact, it is crucial that whenever someone claims to know exactly what a particular culture entails, that this knowledge is questioned, or to check whether women in the same community describe the content of that culture in the same way. For that, it is crucial not only to build up contacts with (male) political and local/community leadership, but to also include experiences of those working with grass root organisations. In practice this means that an exchange of experiences and knowledge about a culture takes place between e.g. embassy personnel and development workers (often working for independent agencies, funded by foreign governments who subsidise development co-operation projects). Another method may be to look at all initiatives by local women's or other groups, no matter how small or well-established, and analyse what they are working on (e.g. on violence, on alcoholism, on community organising). It is important to have a good picture of their working methods and their approaches. What concepts/values or terminology do they use (e.g. disturbance of the harmony of the family, disruption of the community)? Next this terminology may also be used by external (of foreign affairs) governmental officials or other actors in this field when speaking with community leaders and internal government representatives. They thereby will have included women's voices. They also stand a good chance of improving the dialogue with these representatives because the latter may well understand this moral language from their own communities.

An example of this process comes from the Oxfam Novib experience in a project in Mexico. "While enrolled in a development training project, the female participants' continuous weaving drew attention. A small research project was undertaken on the women's collective weaving, which was done by a few indigenous women. It appeared that weaving had a symbolic, cosmologic meaning and provided women with symbolic power. The knowledge about this meaning had become diluted. However, it was felt important to use this meaning as an empowering tool."[60] This story shows the importance of listening to local women and grasping the images and the terminology in which they express themselves, to find out where their concerns lie, and how they voice these concerns.

SUPPORTING RELIGIOUS WOMEN IN THEIR STRUGGLE FOR INTERNAL CHANGE

Religious women may view their religion primarily in terms of virtue and piety, involving submission or "the desire to be controlled by an authority external to oneself". If we are to think seriously about women's agency, we may have to "detach the notion of agency from the goals of progressive politics" and query the presumed opposition between *submission* and *agency*.[61] Religious women should thus be accorded the same *respect* as non-religious women. But this ethical stance should not dismiss political questions and put religious commands beyond the realm of discussion and negotiation of whether they affect women's human rights and opportunities.

All religious traditions have troubles in finding their proper response to the effects of radical changes in public opinion about gender and morals. Traditional religious establishments tend to view feminist agendas and the notion of gender[62] as the greatest threat not only to their religious traditions and their moral authoritative claims, but also to what they hold as a sacred or divinely ordained natural order, inscribed in their moral codes. This perceived threat has mobilised reactive movements in all religious traditions. Women's bodies and sexuality have thus reappeared as a political site of claiming difference and of resistance to homogenising and egalitarian forces.

It must be remembered that, similar to culture at large, all religions have static 'everlasting' aspects, but at the same time are dynamic as well. Although they vary in the degree and nature of their dynamism, they are defined at least in some ways by their members' goals and objectives in life. The history of Christianity, which now has many different well established 'teachings' or 'churches', is exemplary for this. Many authors stress that, for example, also Islam is not a homogenous belief system. Rather it is an extremely complex and

---

60 Oral information by anthropologist Jeanette Kloosterman, Oxfam Novib.

61 Philips 2009, p 42.

62 This is because gender is defined as a human construction, and therefore changeable, and not as something with an everlasting content.

multifaceted phenomenon that has been the subject of numerous, often violent, disagreements among its adherents.[63]

In the last decades in all major religions women themselves have begun to seriously challenge the established patriarchal images and the exclusively male control over those images. Exciting and heated debates occur within all traditions, and this has resulted in a "global expansion of female religious subjectivity and agency".[64] As Madhavi Sunder states it evocatively: "On the ground, women in the Muslim world are piercing the veil of sovereignty."[65] However, this observation should not lead us to exaggerate what can be achieved by internal reform alone. "The difficulty is that internal reform is hardest to mobilise precisely where there is most need for it. The religions whose practices are currently most problematic for gender equality will be the very ones that block women or homosexuals from organising internal change."[66] Therefore, a combination of internal reform and external pressure, by the State or by civil society organisations, seems to harvest the best results.

With regard to possibilities for internal religious change two aspects need to be clear. Firstly, it has been found that the vitality of internal reform may depend on what is happening externally, or at the level of the State. For example, the strong support for gender equality by religious intellectuals in Iran in the 1990s was enabled by the weakening conservative power and the relatively liberal presidencies of Khatami.[67] Where the rights of women are accorded more weight in a country's politics and legislation, the prospects for internal religious reform are much enhanced.

The second aspect is that internal reform movements may use a problematic distinction between religion and culture, even though it may be highly effective for their reform purposes. They may separate what are accepted as genuine religious requirements from the merely cultural accretions, embracing the first and repudiating the latter. But in this way, one may become entangled in the problem of whether later modifications of religion – that may be more egalitarian – are valid or only the 'original' ones. Current religious fundamentalist movements precisely wish to cast away later, more 'degenerate' forms. The separation of 'real' religion from its cultural accretions is a political, therefore always contestable, act. It also implies that if discriminatory and repugnant

63 An-Na'im 1990, p 359.
64 Casanova 2009, p 25.
65 Sunder 2003, Afary 2004, p 114 and further.
66 Philips 2009, p 52. The book of Dutch journalist Rob Vreeken 2010 provides many illustrations of emancipation within Muslim countries. The title is exemplary: 'Boss in one's own belly. From Qur'an to girlpower' (translated from the original Dutch title).
67 Philips 2009, p 52.

practices would be identified as a foundational part of the religion, derived from a holy book or a foundational spiritual leader, then no further questions or critiques would be allowed. Though frequently held, such a view may block internal reform.[68] As Narayan argues, claims about what are core defining values in any particular religion or culture are routinely deployed to immunise those practices that are most to the disadvantage of women from internal or external critique.[69]

AVOIDING REVOLUTIONARY OR RADICAL LANGUAGE

In Chapter 3 it was discussed that there is a divide between 'nature' and 'nurture' as far as the perception of actual or factual differences between men and women are concerned, which in turn are reflected in different perceptions of the relations between them: 'nature' seeing sex inequality and patriarchy as a cornerstone of unchangeable cultural institutions (like e.g. the family); 'nurture' taking the stance that all such gender differences are humanly constructed and therefore are subject to change in the direction of more equality for women. In that Chapter we have also discussed that the construction of culture and gender are deeply related to the formation of group identity, national identity and personal identity and to the construction of the 'natural' family.

Usage of the term 'gender' may already evoke strong resistance from representatives of those cultures in which the presumed natural role of women is very central to their understanding of their identity and of the true relations between the sexes.[70] Any suggestion that this gender identity is constructed may lead to great anxiety. Such resistance, in many cases, may simply be avoided by using the term 'sex equality' (instead of 'gender equality'), meaning that *biological* males and females have a fundamental right to equal treatment. In each instance where actual biological differences with respect to childbearing and childrearing are *not* at stake, such equal treatment on the ground of sex is indicated.[71] Other than biological differences between men and women are the result of 'nurture', i.e. are constructed within the context of a particular culture. In discussions about women's human rights it should be clarified that such constructed differences may not be used as a basis for denying women the enjoyment of these rights. It is not always necessary or advisable to use words like 'gender' or 'gender

68 Philips 2009, p 53.

69 Uma Narayan 1998.

70 Exemplary for this is the fierce political struggle, during the 4th World Conference in Beijing, to include the word gender in the final document. Strong resistance came from especially Catholic and Islamic countries.

71 Below we discuss the opposite situation, where actual biological differences between the sexes may call for a difference in treatment between them.

equality' in that respect. The language of (formal) sex equality is often more appropriate and effective.

This is certainly the case with the most basic political and civil human rights of women: the right to property, the right to vote, the right to physical and moral integrity, the right to marry a person of free choice, the right not to be subjugated to unfair trial, et cetera. There is no point in talking about *gender* equality in these areas. The formal legal right to equality of the sexes should prevail in respect to all of these fundamental human rights.[72] One may also avoid the term sex equality. This may be wise because the other may mistakenly think you are talking about sexual behaviour, while that is of course not the case. Instead, one may choose to talk about legal equality as such. The constitutive idea behind equality in / of the law[73] is that *any* categorisation between human beings in law should have a rational basis. Any legal categorisation should have an *objective justification*. This means: any categorisation between citizens that are subjects of the law should reflect a *real and relevant difference* between them. The consequences of all legal categorisations (which are used as a basis for giving or withholding rights or opportunities to certain categories of people) should be proportionate to the actual differences between people, and should be appropriate and necessary to reach the policy objective of the particular legal rule.

For example: if a government wants to achieve the aim of providing social benefits to the unemployed in order to protect them from starving as a consequence of losing their income after a dismissal, the categorisation within the social benefits legislation must be 'fit' to reach that aim. Withholding unemployment benefits to women, as happened in the past in many Western social security systems as a result of breadwinnership provisions, is an example of a 'misfit' in this respect. It means that a particular group of unemployed persons is denied the protection of the law for no other reason than their sex and marital status.

All governments are familiar with this general principle of legality, although they often are not prepared to apply it to women. The discussion in that case should be about the question of whether there is indeed a *real* biological or physical difference between men and women which justifies a particular difference in treatment / rights. That means that one has to engage in the 'nurture versus nature' debate. It means that reliable scientific knowledge of the actual differences between the sexes should be disseminated and discussed. A parallel with discussions about the nature or nurture of racial differences may work as an

72 See also para. 2.2, where we have discussed that CEDAW encompasses three conceptualisations of the principle of equality: formal, substantive and transformative.

73 By some this is called the principle of legality as such. Others sometimes call it the general principle of proportionality.

eye opener in this respect. Especially most formerly colonised people are sensitive to the argument that in the 19th and the beginning of the 20th century racist theories – on the basis of persistent and denigrating stereotypes, bias and prejudice – assigned 'real' psychological, physical or emotional, differences to the different races, often purely on the basis of colour of skin or other physical appearances. These differences were used to legitimise severe forms of discrimination against particular 'other' or minority races. However, since then scientific research has shown that all this is false theory. Something similar has happened and continues to happen to women. Most of the stereotypes about the presumably real differences between men and women have proven to be false stereotypes or over-generalisations of statistical differences. (See para. 3.2.)

LEAVING ROOM FOR DIFFERENTIAL TREATMENT ON THE GROUND OF SEX

Similar to the word 'gender', the word 'equality' may sometimes invoke strong cultural resistance. Very often, opponents to women's equality presume that acceptance of this principle will leave no room for any differential treatment between men and women. It should be clarified that this is a wrong interpretation of this fundamental legal principle. In cases where factual biological differences between the sexes are indeed at stake, a difference in treatment of men and women may not only be allowed, but may in fact be called for.[74] Such unequal treatment is not contrary to the principle of equality between men and women but may be seen as an elaboration of the same principle. The formal and the substantive principles of equality *require* that different situations are treated differently in accordance with their actual difference.[75] Implementation of the principle of equality between men and women therefore does not mean that for example special health care facilities for pregnant women, or maternity leave for women who have recently given birth to a child, would not be possible anymore.[76] The principle of equality also leaves space for temporary special measures in order to overcome the detrimental effects of past discrimination against women, and to offer women the social support which is needed to effectively have equal opportunities in life.[77] With regard to ending discrimination against groups of people who are the victim of stereotyping and

74 See CEDAW Article 4(2).

75 This is the Aristotelian principle, which is central to the idea of legal equality: equal cases must be treated equally and different cases must be treated differently in accordance with their difference. Treating different situations differently may lead to enhancing *de facto* equality when the different treatment is aimed at taking away the obstacles to equal opportunities.

76 See Article 4(2) of CEDAW.

77 See Article 4(1) of CEDAW and CEDAW GR 25.

stigmatisation, the difference principle is at least as important as the principle of (legal) equality. Recognising and respecting difference is an important principle, where it creates space for people who do not want to conform to culturally defined 'identities', like for example the identity of a housewife or mother. Or, as was stated the South African case in which the rights of homosexuals were at stake: "What becomes normal in an open society, then, is not an imposed and standardized form of behaviour that refuses to acknowledge difference, but the acceptance of the principle of difference itself."[78]

SPEAKING OF HUMAN DIGNITY BESIDES EQUALITY

In the discussion about women's human rights it should be underlined that *two* main principles underlie the human rights paradigm: the principles of equality in rights and the principle of human dignity.[79] Women's human dignity may sometimes be a more appropriate 'gate opener' for a dialogue than their (formal and legal) equality. In our description of gender stereotypes we have recalled that in many cultures around the world not only negative (dehumanising or limiting) stereotypes about women exist, but also a great many benevolent stereotypes. Women's reproductive and nurturing capacities are often put on a high pedestal. While acknowledging (and being beware of) the fact that such stereotypes may have restrictive and damaging impacts on women's (perceived) identity and their possibilities in life, they may also be used in a positive way to acknowledge that women's dignity is indeed respected within the culture at hand. In other words: they prove that the concept of women's dignity is already well known in that culture. Next it becomes crucial to apply this concept in areas where it has not yet been applied, as for example in the area of women's right to physical integrity (for example, the right not to be battered by their husbands) or in the area of women's health (for example, the right not to be subjected to degrading or damaging 'medical' treatment).

SEEKING A COMMON MORAL LANGUAGE

It has been explained in this book that the concept of human rights is based on a *humanistic* value basis. Often it is said that this value basis is Western, implicating

---

[78] South African Supreme Court 1999 1 SA 6 (CC), *National Coalition for Gay and Lesbian Equality vs Ministry of Justice*, para. 143, as quoted by Bonthuys & Albertyn 2007, p 28.

[79] Equality and dignity are explicitly mentioned in the Human Rights Conventions. Underlying these principles is the idea that human beings are autonomous and free beings. Therefore, sometimes people speak of three fundamental principles of human rights: autonomy (or freedom), equality and dignity. See e.g. Baer 2010 (refering to Baer 2009), p 75: "Therefore, I suggest employing an understanding of human rights based on equality, liberty and dignity, in a triangulated perspective of recognition."

that it is not compatible with other value systems.[80] Above (in para. 4.2.) it has already been argued that there exist some fundamental misconceptions of the idea of human rights, being rejected by some cultural or political leaders because of its presumed egocentric, individualistic and irresponsible nature. Whenever this argument is made in a discussion about women's human rights, it should be set straight that this is not true. Human rights do indeed (also) respect and protect the family and the cultural and religious communities and they do acknowledge that individual human beings not only have rights but also have responsibilities in that regard. On the other hand, it is good to ask the question to one's discussion partner why he/she should bother about the perseverance of the family or the community when this is not for the wellbeing of the members? In other words: also those people that defend family values or cultural values as opposed to individualism, often do this with a view to the welfare and prosperity of the individual members of the family or the community. This means that individuals are not seen purely as a means to preserve the community, but are also seen as ends in themselves.

In relation to this misinterpretation of the nature of human rights, a possible strategy could be to loosen oneself a bit from the predominant 'rights language' of the legal human rights discourse, and to look for moral codes or moral values which are recognised by both sides participating in the dialogue.[81] This means, to use other communications than the human *rights* language to express the same principles of equality in rights and respect for human dignity. In a recent UN Report this strategy was described as follows:

> "When human rights education is based on the appreciation of local culture, it expands the capacity of communities to pursue their own basic values and aspirations more coherently. Since these values and ideals tend to be consistent with universal human rights principles, the process does not undermine traditional values but rather adds new dimensions to the discussion. The discussion does not focus on the "eradication" of "bad" traditions, but instead focuses on building a positive vision of girls and women, encouraging their active role in society and enabling them to maintain their traditional values without being subjected to female genital mutilation/cutting. Individuals are not rejecting the bad, but are embracing the good. When the value-based discourse is associated with public commitments that encompass appropriate social networks, it can leverage massive collective change."[82]

Language and arguments, invoked from the local cultural communities, may suit to give an increased legitimacy and support to change discriminatory

80 E.g. Polis & Schwab 1979.

81 See also Nyamu 2000, p 415, who recommends to invoke a community's own general principles of fairness and justice.

82 UN Secretary General, 'The Girl Child', UN Doc A/64/315, 21 August 2009, para. 70.

perceptions, norms and practices.[83] For example, in the fight against serious violations of women's and girls right to physical integrity in Africa, grass root organisations have deployed a moral language that connected to the value systems of local stakeholders, and thereby were successful in combating traditional practices like female genital mutilation.[84] In that way bridges could be build between local values and human rights values.

SOME EXAMPLES OF COMMON MORAL CONCEPTIONS

It has proven to be possible to successfully use the languages of 'the best interest of the child', 'the principle of reciprocity' or 'avoiding the infliction of pain'. An example of the first is to be found in recent positive experiences in the process of transforming local African cultures in which female genital mutilation or genital cutting was practised on large scale:

> "Within practising communities, the fundamental moral norm of doing the best for one's children motivates a parent's decision to perform the procedure since failure to comply risks the daughter's marriageability and brings shame to her and her family. It is this same moral norm that motivates parents to stop cutting, once the possibility of co-ordinating on a better alternative is introduced by credible figures in a credible manner in the community. When community members discuss and debate alternative perspectives, this moral norm becomes explicit. When integrated with principles of human rights and social justice, the process is transformative."[85]

A second possibility is to refer to the universal principle of reciprocity, the principle that one should concede to the other person whatever one claims for oneself. According to this principle, human rights are those rights that a person would claim for herself or himself and must therefore be conceded to all other human beings.[86] This argument may be made in any case where it is observed that a double standard is being employed by participants to the dialogue, e.g. by claiming for themselves that their cultural rights be observed, but denying the applicability or validity of women's human rights. In the same vein, one could also argue along the lines of the 'golden rule' principle[87]: people should not do to others what they don't want to happen to themselves; for example: they should

83 Nyamu 2000, 405; UNFPA 'State of World Population 2008'. See also Gerry Mackie & John LeJeune 2009.

84 See Mackie & LeJeune 2009 and the Report of the UN Secretary General, 'The Girl Child', UN Doc A/64/315, 31 August 2009, paras 64 and 68.

85 Ibid, para. 69.

86 An-Na'im 1990, p 366.

87 According to many ethical and moral systems of beliefs or philosophies, this golden rule is one of the most fundamental ones in human relations.

not withhold food or healthcare to women and let them starve or die, when they claim these goods and services for themselves.

A third possibility may be to use the concepts of 'harm', 'pain' or 'injury' and seek for local moral codes or values that are based on the rejection of inflicting harm, pain or injury on another human being. Often, such values are shared by both men and women in the cultural community. However, many men have never realised that their behaviour may inflict harm, pain or injury on women. When they beat up 'their own' woman, it is 'for her own good'. An example we came across is the production of a *Manual on Sexual Violence* in Congo, discussing Roman Catholic and traditional views on women and men, and focusing on injustice and harm to women. In addition, training workshop were held with the involvement of representatives of religious groups. This programme was run by women's groups that also provided shelter and medical health care to female victims of sexual violence and was very successful in bringing across the human rights values at stake.[88]

FOCUSING ON OTHER ISSUES THAN WOMEN'S HUMAN RIGHTS

Similar to the case of avoiding the 'rights language', it sometimes is strategically more effective to avoid advocating for the implementation of women's human rights, but to concentrate on other vital issues, like for example economic development, the protection of the environment, or improving conditions of health and health care. Although human rights are seen by some commentators as a "powerful discourse to promote women's status"[89], it is also acknowledged by many that it often evokes a lot of counter arguments, because it is been perceived of as neo colonialist or as typically Western. This is especially the case when the discourse of promoting women's human rights in fact entails a fundamental "critique of culture that marginalises poor and rural people or immigrants" and thus "runs the risk of replicating colonial discourses".[90] From that perspective, it might be more productive not to mention women's human rights or not to put any emphasis on that issue, but to view "(...) problems as caused by poverty, warfare, displacement, and governmental crisis instead of

---

88 Supported by Dutch Catholic Justice and Peace Commission, and development agencies Cordaid and CMC-*Mensen met een Missie*. See Justine Masika Bhamba, the 2008 Dutch Human Rights Award winner and her organization *'Femmes pour les Victims des Violences Sexuelles'* co-operates with this project.

89 Merry 2006, p 100.

90 Ibid.

cultural beliefs and practices."[91] In other words, it is argued that is more sensible and productive to adopt and propagate a development approach instead of a human rights approach.[92]

However useful this strategy might appear at first sight, we tend to be a bit less enthusiastic about it than about the ones we previously discussed in this Chapter. The reason for this is that one can never expect to enter a process of fundamental transformation of existing unequal and oppressive gender relations when this phenomenon is not properly revealed and named as one of the principle causes of persistent discrimination against women and of the continuing gross violations of their human rights.[93] The reason why we think that the existence of Article 5 CEDAW is of such vital importance for the advancement of women's position and their empowerment, is that this provision addresses gender stereotypes and fixed parental gender roles as the root causes of women's oppression and calls for their modification. A strategy where persistent and severe discrimination against women is blamed on other factors, like poverty, internal war or rebellion, or on the unstable political environment, is not revealing but hiding these causes.[94] Therefore, we tend to agree with the Dutch government's policy not to blame poverty for the violations of women's human rights, but to blame such violations for creating and sustaining poverty.[95]

A middle way may be to integrate the development approach with a strong human rights advocacy approach. Such an approach nowadays is often called 'mainstreaming'. This approach confronts the fact that violations of women's human rights are not solely cultural, but that such violations may have multiple causes. Economic deprivation, globalisation of unrestricted capitalism, undemocratic governments, lack of access to justice, bad governance, corruption, internal armed conflicts; all of that may contribute to sustaining the situation of gross violations of women's human rights. When this is recognised and exposed,

---

91 Ibid. See also the argument made by Merry that the CEDAW Committee runs the danger of 'enculturaling' the problem of discrimination against women.

92 See also para. 1.3.

93 Cook & Cusack 2010, p 45 ff, stress the necessity of revealing gender stereotypes in order to open up space for change. Making stereotypes visible (bringing the deep see fish to the surface in order for it to see that there is something more than water!) is a first step in recognizing that unequal gender relations are constructed, i.e. that they are changeable.

94 One might also argue the other way around: putting too much emphasis on cultural causes of discrimination against women may hide the unequal economic and political (power) relations, which lie at the basis of women's discrimination. See e.g. Otto 1997, p 15, who argues that the debate about universality or cultural relativity of human rights in fact "functions as a means of obscuring the issues of power and depoliticizing the struggle for economic dominance that is taking place." See also Merry 2006, who talks about enculturaling the issue of women's human rights.

95 Dutch Policy paper 'Human dignity for all. A human rights strategy for foreign policy', (November2007), p 43. Submitted to Parliament on 5 November 2007 (TK 31 263 no. 1).

it becomes more difficult 'to blame 'other' cultures for bad behaviour'.[96] An example of such an integrated approach can be found in a project on improving the livelihood of the rural population in Egypt. Farmer Field Schools were established in Fayoum with financial support of The Netherlands. Half of the expected 30.000 participants are female. In non-formal groups the participants of the project tackle a broad set of development issues, such as health, education, economic and other issues, in an empowering mode. Gender relationships and perceptions are systematically included in discussions and information campaigns about these development issues.[97]

4.4 SOME FINAL REMARKS

The bottom line of discussions about the position of women in relation to culture is clear: cultural practices which lead to violations of women's human rights are not acceptable. This conclusion is backed up by many statements of international organs, who all unambiguously pronounce that women's human rights take priority over culture. However: it is not enough just to confront the other party with this obligation under international law. Much more can be achieved when – together with other stakeholders, like national NGOs and international organisations – a government in its human rights policies enhances a (careful and sustainable) process of cultural change through intercultural or cross-cultural dialogue, both at the national level (internally) and at the international level.

In order to engage into a fruitful dialogue about women's human rights and culture, the participants in such a dialogue need to have a deep understanding of the background of their own position. From the side of people who advocate for the implementation of women's human rights, this means that using human rights as a buzz word or as a container myth, without fully understanding (and being able to talk about or explain) the historical, philosophical, political and legal meaning of this term, may work counterproductively.

There are many misunderstandings about the nature and content of human rights. One of the most persistent ones is that the basic values underlying human rights are inherently opposed to the core values that are embedded in certain cultures, traditions, customs or religions. This misunderstanding is voiced both by spokesmen or leaders of traditionalist cultures and by advocates of women's human rights. Human rights are said to be individualistic, only having an eye for the rights of the individual to the detriment of the family or the community.

96 Volpp 2000.

97 Oral and written information of Susan Blankhart, Ambassador of the Netherlands in Egypt.

This is not true. Therefore, it should be explained that human rights in fact are *humanistic*; i.e. that they take the *full human being* into account, including his/her close ties to family, community, nation, religion or more generally, to culture. Instead of focussing solely on the *individual rights strategy* (i.e.: helping individual women to claim their human rights in court cases), adopting a more holistic approach to the implementation of human rights which includes a *strategy of social support* and a *strategy for social and cultural change*, will emphasise this *humanistic* instead of the purely *individualistic* basis of human rights. Yes, human rights are based on the inherent (equal) value of each and every individual human being; but no: the individual human being does not have an existence and does not have opportunities to lead a full and meaningful life without the support and care of the family, the community and the nation to which he/she belongs.

Another problem is that it is simply not enough to point out the obligatory nature of internationally agreed human rights standards. Accepting interference with so-called internal affairs by other States and accountability in that regard, requires a long process. Such interference is most difficult to accept when a country's culture (and consequently its national identity) is at stake. Any government needs not only legal and political legitimisation, but also cultural legitimisation for (enhancing) fundamental societal change. But even when States are willing to co-operate, they are themselves quite powerless when they do not find or create the necessary *internal* cultural legitimisation for fundamental change. Instead of bluntly holding a State responsible and accountable for not implementing international human rights standards, CEDAW included, it might be more fruitful to find ways to support them to create a firm basis for this cultural legitimisation for fundamental legal, social-economic and cultural changes as regards transforming the unequal relations between men and women.

One of the key obligations under international human rights law is the obligation – according to Article 5 CEDAW – to address prevailing gender relations and the persistence of gender-based stereotypes. In order for States to start working toward this goal, a deeper understanding of the causes and consequences of discrimination of women is necessary. Therefore, in this book, we have explained to some detail what this aspect of culture means; i.e. how culture gives meaning and structure to gender and how both culture and gender are subsequently being 'essentialised'. From that analysis, lessons can be derived as to who are stakeholders in maintaining and supporting the existing unequal gender relations. Without a good understanding of the deep resistances against any cultural change that involves a modification of gender stereotypes and fixed parental gender roles, no real transformation of a society into the direction of more gender equality is possible.

In this final Chapter, we have addressed a number of possible strategies to locate and to take away some of the most persistent resistances against women's equality. A lot of that resistance comes from inside culture; however, a lot of it is in fact aroused from the outside, i.e. from the international community of advocates of women's human rights that often has adopted similar essentialist approaches to universal human rights and to local culture. By presenting the content and scope of women's human rights as universal and thereby as static and not subjected to any interpretation or change, by means of orientalising culture, and by means of calling for the eradication or abolition of certain cultural practices and beliefs, such advocates might do much more harm than good. They supply all the ammunition for beliefs / statements that women's human rights are Western and a form of neo-colonialism or imperialism. They most certainly lead the discussion into a firm deadlock, instead of opening up space for a fruitful dialogue. A fruitful dialogue and enhancing a process of change may also not be expected from those persons who – being afraid of the reproach of neo-colonialism or false universalism – adopt the stance of cultural relativism. This stance is equally essentialist and offers no arguments at all for putting an end to practices and beliefs that are harmful or oppressive for women.

The slow and difficult process of transformation of unequal and oppressive gender relations requires that *all* who are involved in it are prepared to be open and transparent about motives, arguments, interests, values, norms and perspectives that are at stake. This includes human rights advocates, who must not shield themselves behind authoritative international legal texts. "Transformation works both ways, or not at all."[98] We expect that the argumentative strategies and practical approaches that were discussed in this book may indeed contribute to the goal of putting an end to all those practices and belief that inferiorise and dehumanise women. They are perhaps very small first steps, but without these no long journey can be made.

[98] See the motto of this Chapter.

SUMMARY

CHAPTER 1: INTRODUCTION

Severe violations of women's human rights are more and more often openly defended with a call upon religion, tradition or culture. In many instances, this argument is accompanied by some kind of reproach about human rights being a Western concept, or being neo-colonialist or imperialistic. In that situation, it is not at all effective to hold the other party to the internationally agreed human rights legal norms. In this book we discuss the question how a firm deadlock between on the one hand women's human rights and on the other hand culture / tradition / religion can be avoided. *Or, to put it positively:* How can we enhance a fruitful dialogue about women's human rights and culture / tradition / religion?

In searching for answers to this question, we concentrate on the contribution that international human rights law can offer to this discussion. Using the language of international law forms a crucial input in the difficult debate about women's human rights in the light of culture. The book not only discusses theoretical approaches to the relationship between women's human rights and culture, but also presents best practices of strategies for enhancing a dialogue about this issue.

We acknowledge that underdevelopment and poverty are important factors when it comes down to persistent discrimination against women. However, the reverse is also true: promotion of women's human rights may enhance development. Therefore, we concentrate on the human rights approach to gender equality. It is not to be forgotten that human rights include the right to social and economic security, and even the right to development itself.

This book is intended to help all persons who are assigned with the difficult task of finding solid and dissuasive arguments in favour of women's human rights and presenting them in such a way that they will keep the dialogue with their discussion partners going. We expect that the book will be informative for all such actors and that it will also facilitate debates and stimulate an exchange of views and practices on the issue at hand.

Rikki Holtmaat & Jonneke Naber wrote this book on the basis of a research paper that was written in 2009 at the request of the Dutch Ministry of Foreign Affairs. This research was done in the course of a wider project subsidised by this Ministry(DMHO). The authors are independent academics. The content of this book, therefore, does not necessarily reflect the Ministry's viewpoints.

The book presents the results of an analysis of international legal obligations in the area of women's human rights and the right to preserve one's culture, as well as a survey of relevant literature and interviews with resource persons in which they were asked how they deal with the deadlock or enhance a dialogue in this area.

CHAPTER 2: WOMEN'S HUMAN RIGHTS

The Chapter starts of with an exploration of the normative nature and legal stature of human rights in general (para. 2.1). The idea that all human beings are equal in dignity and rights goes back to the (enlightened) value orientation in which the inherent value and freedom of each and every individual human being is put at the very centre of the moral and ethical system of beliefs and practices. The fundamental principle of equality is foundational for the construction of the democratic constitutional State and for the acceptance of basic citizenship rights. For human rights to be acknowledged on the level of international law, States had to accept that there are boundaries to their sovereignty with regard to how they may treat their inhabitants. Next, it had to become accepted that States could hold each other accountable not only for their own behaviour, but also for the bad or oppressive behaviour of citizens among themselves. A whole doctrine of international human rights law was developed, specifying the nature of the rights and obligations in this respect. However, human rights are not a quiet possession; they continue to be part of political struggles over power relations in any society.

Next (para. 2.2) we concentrate on women's human rights in the context of the Convention on the Elimination of All Forms of Discrimination Against Women (CEDAW). CEDAW was adopted in 1979 and entered into force in 1981. The Convention is now (AD 2010) ratified by 186 States. Its implementation is supervised by a Committee of 23 independent experts. The Convention has a wide scope, covering the protection of women's human rights in all areas of life. Its purposes are threefold: to eliminate discrimination in laws and policies, to enhance the improvement of women's conditions of life, and to address prevailing gender relations and the persistence of gender-based stereotypes. These three objectives are related to a comprehensive understanding of the fundamental principle of women's equality as including formal, substantive and transformative equality. Three major strategies should be applied to fully implement this Convention: giving women individual rights to equality (*Individual Rights Strategy*), supporting women to achieve a position of *de facto* equality with men (*Social Support Strategy*), and taking away the structural causes of any such discrimination through a process of social and cultural change (*Strategy of Social and Cultural Change*). As such CEDAW encompasses a holistic understanding of the causes and consequences of women's persistent inequalities and oppression and the strategies that need to be followed to eliminate this discrimination.

For the purpose of this book, the third objective of CEDAW has special relevance and is discussed in depth (in paras 2.3 and 2.4). This objective is expressed in Article 5, which obliges States parties to this Convention to modify gender stereotypes and fixed parental gender roles in order to realise full equality between women and men. The CEDAW Committee has elaborated in great detail the wide variety of cultural practices that are addressed by this Article and has indicated what States parties should do in order to implement it correctly. On the basis of Article 5, the Committee has made it clear that women's human rights cannot be set aside with a call upon culture. A similar approach can be found in official documents of many other international human rights organs.

In order to put women's human rights in perspective to an often claimed right to culture, we have explored to some extent what this latter concept entails (in para. 2.5). In that context, it is important to distinguish clearly between a right of individuals to enjoy their culture and to participate in shaping and expressing it, and a right of cultural groups that their culture be protected, or be sustained or supported. In the framework of human rights discussions, it is a common position not to let the latter (group) right prevail above the first and above other human rights (e.g. women's human right to equality and dignity).

CHAPTER 3: CULTURE AND GENDER

Culture entails such phenomena as language, shared beliefs or ideals, traditional music, national hymns, historical events and heroes, images and art, sports, local customs and traditions, laws, societal organisations and institutions and religion and religious institutions. This broad notion of culture is closely linked to the construction of identity, both on the level of social or ethnic groups or nations or nationality, and on the level of the family and individual men and women. Any culture that leads to a negative, unequal and undignified personal identity of some of its members, in terms of being inferior to other members or being subjugated to their absolute power, contravenes the basic values underlying the notion of human rights for all.

One of the key issues in this Chapter (discussed in para. 3.2) is the nature of the relationship between culture and gender; the latter term referring to the way in which the physical or biological categories of the male and female sex get meaning and structure through culture. Gender stereotypes and fixed parental gender roles are part and parcel of *every* culture on planet earth. With a view to Article 5 CEDAW, we concentrate on those aspects of culture that lead to invidious or harmful gender stereotypes and to fixed parental gender roles that form barriers for women to use all of their human capacities or capabilities and to lead a meaningful life as a human being. Gender stereotypes and fixed parental gender roles are very difficult to change, *inter alia* because people are often unaware of them, but also because they lay the basis for a particular cultural gender identity of individual men and women, of social and cultural groups, as well as of States. It is therefore not feasible to abolish or eradicate them altogether; rather one should strive for their modification, as is the language of Article 5 CEDAW.

Culture is often interpreted and presented in such a way that a clash with the human rights of women becomes (seemingly) unavoidable. Our analysis (in para. 3.3) reveals that a most important obstacle to cultural change, i.e. a change in existing unequal gender relations, is the widely held belief of cultural essentialism. We describe by whom and why this belief is voiced in the debates about women's human rights. It appears that not only people from within particular cultures are of the opinion that their culture is homogenous and static, but that often also people who advocate for human rights exhibit the same opinion. Human rights advocates tend to orientalise culture, soon after which a plea for the eradication or abolishment of 'bad' cultures can be heard. Finally, also adherents to so-called multicultural or cultural relativist perspectives see different (but equal) cultures as having distinctive or essential features.

The final part of this Chapter (para. 3.4) discusses whether there is a special place for religion within culture. Religion is of particular importance for human beings in the construction of a meaning of life. Religious people often have serious objections against capturing religion under the wider notion of culture and subsequently prioritising women's human rights over culture. They argue that culture possibly may be constructed by human beings, but that religion is God-given, or that the content of their belief can be *found* in holy texts, that have an eternal (fixed) meaning. One strategy to counteract such arguments might be to make a distinction between religion as a *spiritual* experience, and its *actual rules and practices.* Another point for consideration is that those who claim an exemption for religion on the basis of the right to religious freedom in fact rely on the same secular legal norms as the ones they reject in the name of religion, i.e. women's human rights.

CHAPTER 4: FROM A FIRM DEADLOCK TO A FRUITFUL DIALOGUE

The final Chapter is dedicated to answering the central question of this book: what are feasible strategies to avoid a firm deadlock and to enhance a fruitful dialogue about women's human rights and culture? After having briefly described who might be the main discussion partners in such a project, we first (in para. 4.1) discuss the necessity and the boundaries of engaging into a dialogue. It is acknowledged by many that the only way out of a deadlock between opposite and fixed positions in the debate about women's human rights and culture is to engage into an intercultural or cross-cultural dialogue. What is meant by that phrase? It should be kept in mind that talking *with* someone is not the same as talking *to* someone or talking *along with* someone. It is therefore necessary to ascertain the bottom line or boundary of any discussion about women's position. Often, this boundary is found in international legal standards concerning women's equal rights.

However, it is far too simple to just say that women's human rights need to be respected *under all circumstances*. There are important structural barriers in that regard, that need to be acknowledged and addressed (as is discussed in para. 4.2). In order for such a call to be possibly effective, the other party should already respect the moral and ethical value orientation underlying these rights. Moreover, it has to accept that international law limits the State's sovereign powers and puts positive obligations on the State party to implement human rights also in horizontal relations. It necessary to acknowledge these preconditions for the implementation of women's human rights, and – if they are not fulfilled – start to realise them. Thus, it is necessary to (help) strengthen the legal and cultural legitimisation of a national government to enhance a fundamental change in the exiting culturally determined unequal gender relations. It also means that advocates of women's human rights must be able to take away some of the most persistent misunderstandings about the normative nature of human rights, for example the idea that they are individualistic and lead to the egocentric, irresponsible behaviour of people which undermines the community and the family. Instead of that, the humanistic value orientation of human rights, which also takes important communitarian values into account, should be explained and exemplified. Human beings are not completely separated or isolated from their family and their cultural community, having only rights and no responsibilities. Many well established human rights fully acknowledge the fact that human beings cannot flourish and exist without the family, religion, language, culture, or tradition.

In the third part of the Chapter (para. 4.3) we describe various possible responses to the 'traditionalist' resistances against cultural change, which reflect the fact that gender is constructed and reproduced on all levels in society and in private life. Gender plays a crucial role in the construction of the identity of groups and nations and of individual men and women. Unequal gender relations lie at the basis of what is perceived of as natural family relations and natural heterosexual sexuality. There are many different stakeholders within a particular culture to maintain this status quo, who will use all possible arguments to prevent any substantial change in this regard. In this section, different strategies to make a dialogue with these stakeholders more feasible are discussed. We (inter alia) talk about recognising vested interests and seeking a win-win situation as well as seeking a safe environment for change. An important stakeholder is the State, who's very national identity may be at stake when unequal gender relations are (supposed to) being changed.

In order to counteract the false impression that women's human rights will automatically lead to an irresponsible and egoistic culture of claiming individual rights, it should be stressed that CEDAW not only calls for giving people access to such rights, but also calls for social support and social and cultural change. In all instances it is important to include women's voices in the dialogue and hear how they phrase their opinions, concerns and commitments. Also it is sometimes better to avoid language that is perceived of as revolutionary or radical (like the language of 'gender' and 'equality'). Instead, it is often more productive to seek for a common moral language that may construct a link between human rights and culture. A final strategy could be to focus on other issues than women's human rights (like e.g. development, environment, or health care) and hope that along the way this will also have a positive effect on women's position. However, this may be deceptive: one can never expect to enter a process of fundamental change of existing unequal gender relations when this phenomenon is not properly revealed and named as one of the principle causes of persistent discrimination of women and of the continuing gross violations of their human rights. A better strategy might be to mainstream gender equality and development.

After a brief summary of the main findings in this book, we conclude (in para. 4.4) with a call upon advocates of women's human rights to stop orientalising culture and to bluntly demanding the abolition or eradication of certain traditional, religious or customary practices. A fruitful dialogue and enhancing a process of cultural change can also not be expected from those who – being afraid of the reproach of neo-colonialism or imperialism – adopt the stance of cultural relativism. This stance is equally essentialist and offers no arguments at all for putting an end to practices and beliefs that are harmful for women. A process of transformation of unequal gender relations means that *all* who are involved in it are prepared to be open and transparent about motives, arguments, interests, values and perspectives that are at stake. We expect that the argumentative strategies and practical approaches that are discussed in this book may indeed contribute to the goal of putting an end to all those practices and belief that inferiorise and dehumanise women. They are perhaps very small first steps, but without these no long journey can be made.

BIBLIOGRAPHY

(NB: Official documents of national and international organisations are not included here; they are fully referenced in the footnotes.)

Afary, Janet, The human rights of Middle Eastern & Muslim women: a project for the 21st century', in: *Human Rights Quarterly*, (2004) 26, pp 106–125.

Alston, Philip & Robinson, Mary: *Human Rights and Development; Towards Mutual Reinforcement*. Oxford: Oxford University Press, 2004.

Alston, Philip, 'Ships Passing in the Night, The Current State of the Human Rights and Development Debate seen Through the Lens of the Millennium Development Goals'; in: *Human Rights Quarterly*, (2005) 27, pp 755–829.

Amaya-Castro, Yuan M., *Human Rights and the Critiques of the Public–Private Distinction*, Amsterdam: Vrije Universiteit (PhD Thesis), 2010.

An-Na'im, Abdullahi A., 'Problems of universal cultural legitimacy', in: An-Na'im, Abdullahi A. & Deng, Francis M. (eds), *Human Rights in Africa. Cross Cultural Perspectives*, New York: Brookings Institution, 1990, pp 331–367.

An-Na'im, Abdullahi A., 'State Responsibility Under International Human Rights law to Change Religious and Customary Laws', in: Cook, Rebecca J. (ed.), *Human Rights of Women; National and International Perspectives*, Philadelphia: University of Pennsylvania Press, 1994, pp 167–188.

Appiah, Kwame Anthony, 'Identity, Authenticity, Survival: Multicultural Societies and Social Reproduction', in: Gutmann, Amy (ed.), *Multiculturalism: Examining "The Politics of Recognition"*, Princeton: Princeton University Press, 1994, pp 149–163.

Appiah, Kwame Anthony, 'Stereotypes and the Shaping of Identity', in: *Californian Law Review*, (2000) 88, pp 41–53.

Asia Pacific Forum on Women, Law and Development (APWLD), *Fundamentalism in Asia-Pacific: trends, impact, challenges and strategies asserting women's rights*, Chiang Mia 2008.

Avdeyeva, Olga, 'When do States comply with international treaties? Policies on violence against women in post-communist countries', in: *International Studies Quarterly*, (2007) 51, pp 877–900.

Baer, Susanne, 'Dignity, Liberty, Equality: A Fundamental Rights Triangle of Constitutionalism', *University of Toronto L.J.*, (2009) pp 417–468.

Baer, Susanne, 'A Closer Look at Law: Human Rights as Multi-level Sites of Struggles over Multi-dimensional Equality', *Utrecht Law Review*, (2010) Vol. 6, issue 2, pp 56–76.

Baretto, Manuela & Ellemers, Naomi, 'The burden of benevolent sexism: how it contributes to the maintenance of gender inequalities', in *European Journal of Social Psychology*, (2005) 35, pp 63–642.

Baretto, Manuela, Ellemers, Naomi, Piebinga, Laura & Moya, Miguel, 'How nice of us and how dumb of me: the effect of exposure to benevolent sexism on women's task and relational self-description'. Unpublished paper; made available to the author by Prof. Naomi Ellemers, University of Leiden.

Beauvoir, Simone de, *The second sex*, 1952. Edition: Howard M. Parshley (trans. and ed.), New York: Alfred A. Knopf, 1989.

Benniger-Budel, Carin (ed): *Due diligence and its application to protect women from violence.* Leiden-Boston: Martinus Nijhoff Publishers, 2008.

Berger, Maurits, *Religion and Development Aid. The Special Case of Islam*, Clingendael Diplomacy Paper No.8, Netherlands Institute of International Relations The Hague: Instituut Clingendael, 2006.

Bielefeldt, Heiner, 'Autonomy and Republicanism. Immanuel Kant's Philosophy of Freedom', in: *Political Theory*, (1997) Vol. 25, pp 524–558.

Bielefeldt, Heiner, '"Western" versus "Islamic" Human Rights Conceptions? A Critique of Cultural Essentialism in the Discussion on Human Rights', in: *Political Theory*, (2000) Vol 28 (1), pp 90–121.

Boerefijn, Ineke, Coomans, Fons, Goldschmidt, Jenny, Holtmaat, Rikki, & Wolleswinkel, Ria (red.), *Temporary Special Measures; Accelerating de facto equality of women under article 4(1) UN Convention on the Elimination of all forms of Discrimination Against Women.* Antwerpen / Oxford / New York: Intersentia, 2003.

Boerefijn, Ineke, 'Women's right to political participation. The case of the Reformed Political Party in The Netherlands', in: Holtmaat, Rikki & Boerefijn, Ineke (eds) *Women's Human Rights and Culture/Religion/Tradition: International Standards as Guidelines for the Discussion?* Proceedings of the Colloquium in the Peace Palace, the Hague 12 May 2009. Utrecht: SIM Special (2010), no. 32, pp 121–139.

Brink, Marjolein van den, 'Gendered sovereignty? In search of gender bias in the international law concept of state sovereignty', in: Boerefijn, I., Goldschmidt, J. (eds), *Changing perceptions of sovereignty and human rights. Essays in honour of Cees Flinterman*, Antwerp: Intersentia, 2008, pp 65–83.

Butegwa, Florence, 'Mediating Culture and Human Rights in Favour of Land Rights for Women in Africa: A Framework for Community-level Action', in: An-Na'im, Abdullah A. (ed), *Cultural Transformation and Human Rights in Africa*, London: Zed Books, 2002.

Butler, Judith, *Gender Trouble; Feminism and the Subversion of Identity*, London: Routledge, 1990.

Casanova, José, 'Religion, politics and gender equality: Public religions revisited', in: Casanova, José & Phillips, Anne, *A Debate on the Public Role of Religion and its Social and Gender Implications.* Programme on Gender and Development, Paper No. 5. Geneva: UNRISD, 2009, pp 7–28.

Chodorow, Nancy, *Feminism and Psychoanalytic Theory*, New Haven: Yale University Press, 1989.

Clark, Ann Marie, *Diplomacy of Conscience. Amnesty International and changing human rights norms*, Princeton: Princeton University Press, 2001.

Cook, Rebecca J. & Cusack, Simone, *Gender stereotyping; Transnational Legal Perspectives*, Philadelphia: University of Pennsylvania Press, 2010.

Cornell, Drucilla, *Transformations: Recollective Imagination and Sexual Difference*, New York: Routledge 1993.

Crenshaw, Kimberlé, 'Demarginalizing the Intersection of Race and Sex, a Black Feminist Critique of Antidiscrimination Doctrine, Feminist Theory, and Antiracist Politics', in: (1989) *University of Chicago Legal Forum* (Special Issue: Feminism in the Law: Theory, Practice and Criticism). Reprinted in: Bartlett, Katharine T. & Kennedy, Rosanne (eds.), *Feminist Legal Theory*, Boulder/San Francisco/Oxford: Westview Press, 1991, pp 57–80.

Cusack, Simone & Cook, Rebecca J., 'Combating Discrimination on Sex and Gender, in: Krause, Catarine & Scheinin, Martin (eds.), in: *International Protection of Human Rights: A textbook*, Institute for Human Rights, Abo Akademi Univeristy 2009, pp 205–226.

Delphy, Christine, 'Antiseksisme of antiracisme? Een vals dilemma', in: *Tijdschrift voor Genderstudies* (2009), 12–1, pp 54–66; also published as: 'Antisexisme *ou* antiracisme? Un faux dilemme.' in: *Nouvelle Questions Feministes*, Vol 25, 1, pp. 59–83.

Dipo-Salami, Bunmi & Assefa, Emrakeb, *Gender mainstreaming and transformative female leadership development: voices from Ethiopia*, Oxfam Novib evaluation, 2008 (on file with authors).

Donders, Y.M., *Towards a Right to Cultural Diversity?* Antwerpen: Intersentia, 2002.

Donders, Yvonne, 'Assepoester vindt haar prins; De onafhankelijke deskundige culturele rechten', *NJCM-bulletin* (2009)34–7, pp 811–828.

Ferreira, Monica, 'Elder abuse in Africa: what policy and legal provisions are there to address the violence?', in: *Journal of elder abuse and neglect*, (2004) Vol. 16 – 2, pp 17–32.

Fiske, Susan T., et al., "Social science research on trial: The use of sex stereotyping research in *Price Waterhouse v. Hopkins*", in: *American Psychologist*, (1991), 46, pp 1049–1060.

Flinterman, Cees, 'Reservations to CEDAW', in: Holtmaat, Rikki & Boerefijn, Ineke (eds), *Women's Human Rights and Culture/Religion/Tradition: International Standards as Guidelines for the Discussion?* Proceedings of the Colloquium in the Peace Palace, the Hague 12 May 2009. Utrecht: SIM Special (2010) nr. 32, pp 53–60.

Fontanelli, Filippo, Martinico, Giuseppe & Carrozza, Paolo (eds), *Shaping Rule of Law Through Dialogue. International and Supranational Experiences*, Groningen: European Law Publishing, 2009.

Fortman, Bas de Gaay, 'Mensenrechten in de internationale oecumene: de dialectiek van idee en project', in: Naber, Jonneke (ed), *Verslag van een beraadsdag over christelijk geloof en mensenrechten*, Oegstgeest: Werkgroep Mensenrechten Raad van Kerken, 1997, pp 21–27.

Francioni, F. & Scheinin, M. (eds), *Cultural Human Rights*, Leiden: Martinus Nijhoff Publishers, 2008.

Fredman, Sandra, 'Beyond the dichotomy of formal and substantive equality. Towards new definitions of equal rights', in: Boerefijn, I., Coomans, F., Goldschmidt, J., Holtmaat, R. & Wolleswinkel, R. (eds.), *Temporary special measures. Accelerating de facto equality of women under article 4(1) UN Convention on the Elimination of all forms of Discrimination Against Women*, Antwerp/Oxford/New York: Intersentia 2003, pp 111–118.

Galenkamp, Marlies, *Individualism versus Collectivism; The Concept of Collective Rights*, Rotterdam: Faculteit der Wijsbegeerte, Erasmus University, 1993.

Gherardi, Silvia, 'The Gender We Think, The Gender We Do in Our Everyday Organizational Lives'; in: *Human Relations*, (1994) 47–6, pp 591–610.

Groenman, L.S., Vleuten, C.E. van, Holtmaat, R., Dijk, T.E. van & Wildt, J.H.J. de (Groemnan et al), *Het vrouwenverdrag in Nederland anno 1997*, Den Haag: Ministerie van SZW 1997. (First Dutch Independent Expert Report on the basis of Article 3 of the Law According the Ratification of CEDAW.).

Gross, A.M., 'Sex, 'Love, and Marriage; Questioning Gender and Sexuality Rights in International Law', in: *Leiden Journal of International Law*, (2008) 21, pp 235–253.

Gunning, Isabelle, 'Arrogant Perception, World Travelling and Multicultural Feminism: the Case of Female Genital Surgeries', in: *Columbia Human Rights Law Review*, (1992) 23, pp 189–238.

Gutmann, Amy (ed.), *Multiculturalism: Examining "The Politics of Recognition"*, Princeton: Princeton University Press, 1994.

Hamburger, Arjan, 'Opening Address, in: Holtmaat, Rikki & Boerefijn, Ineke (eds), *Women's Human Rights and Culture/Religion/Tradition: International Standards as Guidelines for the Discussion?* Proceedings of the Colloquium in the Peace Palace, the Hague 12 May 2009. Utrecht: SIM Special (2010) no. 32, pp 9–13.

Hawkins, Darren, "Explaining costly international institutions: persuasion and enforceable human rights norms", in: *International Studies Quarterly*, (2004) 48, pp 779–804.

Heringa, A.W., Hes, J., Lijnzaad, E. (eds.), *Het Vrouwenverdrag. Een beeld van een verdrag*, Antwerpen/Apeldoorn: Maklu 1994.

Hernández-Truyol, Berta Esperanza, "Out of the shadows: traversing the imaginary of sameness, difference, and relationalism – a human rights proposal", in: *Wis. Women's L.J.*, (2002) 17, pp 111–162.

Hes, J.C. & Vleuten, C.E. Van, *Het Vrouwenverdrag in de Nederlandse rechtsorde*, Den Haag: Ministerie SZW 1996.

Hofstadter, Douglas, 'On seeing A's and seeing As', in: *Stanford Humanities Review*, (1995) 4/2, pp 109–121.

Holtmaat, Rikki, 'Gender, the analytical concept that tackles the hidden structural bias of law', in: *Recht Richting Frauen; Beitrage zur feministischen Rechtswisschenschaft*, Lachen/St. Gallen: Dike Verlag, 2001, pp 159–182.

Holtmaat, Rikki, 'Het gelijkheidsbeginsel: van een vat vol dilemma's naar drie typen van gelijkerechtenwetgeving', in: *Gelijkheid en rechtvaardigheid; Staatsrechtelijke vraagstukken rondom 'minderheden'*. Deventer: Kluwer, 2002(a), pp 161–175.

Holtmaat, Rikki, 'De meerwaarde van het Vrouwenverdrag in de multiculturele samenleving', in: Holtmaat, R. (ed.), *Eén Verdrag voor alle vrouwen. Verkenningen van de betekenis van het VN-Vrouwenverdrag voor de multiculturele samenleving*, The Hague: E-Quality, 2002(b), pp 129–145.

Holtmaat, Rikki, 'Building blocks for a General Recommandation on Article 4(1) of the CEDAW Convention. Report of the expert meeting in Maastricht 10–12 October 2002', in: Boerefijn, I., Coomans, F., Goldschmidt, J., Holtmaat, R. en Wolleswinkel,

R. (eds.), *Temporary special measures. Accelerating de facto equality of women under article 4(1) UN Convention on the Elimination of all forms of Discrimination Against Women,* Antwerp/Oxford/New York: Intersentia 2003, p 213–230.

Holtmaat, Rikki, *Towards Different Law and Public Policy; The significance of Article 5a CEDAW for the elimination of structural gender discrimination.* The Hague/ Doetinchem: Reed Business Information, 2004 (out of print, but to be downloaded from: www.rikkiholtmaat.nl/Towards_Different_Law_and_Public_Policy.pdf).

Holtmaat, Rikki, 'Preventing Violence Against Women; The Due Diligence Standard and Article 5(a) CEDAW,' in: Benninger-Budel, Carin (ed.), *Due Diligence and its Application to Protect Women from Violence,* Martinus Nijhoff Publishers, Leiden-Boston 2008, p 225–239.

Holtmaat, Rikki, 'Article 5 CEDAW and Culture, Religion and Tradition.' In: Holtmaat, Rikki & Boerefijn, Ineke (eds), *Women's Human Rights and Culture/Religion/ Tradition: International Standards as Guidelines for the Discussion?* Proceedings of the Colloquium in the Peace Palace, the Hague 12 May 2009. Utrecht: SIM Special (2010) no. 32, pp 15–40.

Holtmaat, Rikki, 'Article 5'; Chapter 7 in: Freeman, Chinkin & Rudolf (eds), *The Convention on the Elimination of all forms of Discrimination Against Women; A Commentary.* Oxford: Oxford University Press 2011 (forthcoming).

Holtmaat, Rikki & Tobler, Christa, 'CEDAW and the European Union's Policy in the Field of Combating Gender Discrimination', in: *Maastricht Journal of European and Comparative Law,* (2005) 4, pp. 399–425.

Holtmaat, Rikki & Boerefijn, Ineke (eds), *Women's Human Rights and Culture/Religion/ Tradition: International Standards as Guidelines for the Discussion?* Proceedings of the Colloquium in the Peace Palace, the Hague 12 May 2009. Utrecht: SIM Special (2010), no. 32.

Houtepen, Anton, 'From freedom of religion towards a really free religion', in: Naber, Jonneke (ed), *Freedom of Religion: a Precious Human Right,* Assen: Van Gorcum, 2000, pp 43–53.

Jagger, Alison, *Feminist Politics and Human Nature,* New Jersey: Rowman & Alanheld 1983.

Kaviraj, Sudipta, 'Universality and the Inescapability of History: How Universal is a Declaration of Human Rights', in: May, Hans & Oppermann, Sybille Fritsch (eds), *Menschenrechte zwischen Universalisierungsanspruch und kultureller Kontextualisierung, Loccumer Protokolle 10/93,* Rehberg-Loccum, Germany: Evangelische Akademie Loccum, (1993), pp 75–96.

Koukoulis-Spiliotopoulos, Sophia, 'The limits of cultural traditions', in: *Annuaire International des Droits de l'Homme* III, (2008) pp 412–443.

Kymlicka, Will, *Liberalism, Community and Culture,* Oxford: Oxford University Press, 1989.

Lauren, Paul Gordon, *The Evolution of International Human Rights,* Pennsylvania: University of Pennsylvania Press, 1999.

Levy, Jack T., 'Classifying Cultural Rights', in: Shapiro, Ian & Kymlicka, Will, *Ethnicity and group rights,* New York: New York University Press, 1997, pp 22–66.

Lijnzaad, Liesbeth, 'Over rollenpatronen en de rol van het Verdrag', in: Heringa, A.W., Hes, J. & Lijnzaad, E. (ed.), *Het Vrouwenverdrag. Een beeld van een verdrag,* Maklu: Antwerpen/Apeldoorn 1994, p 43–57.

Maarseveen, Henc van, 'Internationaal vrouwenrecht. Een afzonderlijk rechtsgebied?' & 'Hoofdstuk 8: Verwerkelijking', in: Maarseveen, H. Van, Pessers, D. & Gunning, M.J. (eds), *Internationaal recht en vrouwen (Deel 1 Commentaren),* Zwolle: Tjeenk-Willink, 1987, pp 69–80 & pp 135–140.

Mackie, Gerry & LeJeune, John, *Social Dynamics of Abandonment of Harmful Practices*; New York: UNICEF, Innocenti Working Papers Series, 2009 (-06).

Mehra, Madhu, 'Women's Equality and Culture in the Context of Identity Politics', in: *Journal of Comparative Law* (2007) 2:2, pp 6–37.

Menon, Nivedita, 'State, Community and the Debate on the Uniform Civil Code in India', in: Mamdani, Mahmood (ed*), Beyond Rights Talk and Culture Talk: Comparative Essays on the Politics of Rights and Culture*, New York: St. Martin's Press, 2000, pp 75–96.

Merry, Sally Engle, 'Rights talk and the experience of law: implementing women's human rights to protection from violence', in: *Human Rights Quarterly* (2003) 25, pp 343–381.

Merry, Sally Engle, 'Human Rights Law and the Demonization of Culture (And Anthropology Along the Way)', in: *Polar: Political and Legal Anthropology Review*, (2003) Vol 26, no. 1, pp 55–77 (quoted as Merry 2003 Polar).

Merry, Sally Engle, *Human Rights & Gender Violence. Translating international law into local justice*, Chicago: University of Chicago Press, 2006.

Míguez, Daniel, 'Poor people in religiously diverse contexts: assets and drawbacks in the Latin American experience', in: Naber, Jonneke (ed), *Freedom of Religion: a Precious Human Right*, Assen: Van Gorcum, 2000, pp 141–151.

Moore, Sally Falk, *Law as process: an anthropological approach*, Oxford: Oxford University Press, 1978.

Naber, Jonneke (ed), *Freedom of Religion: a Precious Human Right*, Assen: Van Gorcum, 2000.

Narayan, Uma, 'Essence of Culture and a Sense of History: A Feminist Critique of Cultural Essentialism', in: *Hypatia* (1998) vol. 13, no. 2, pp 86–106.

Nhlapo, T., 'The African Customary Law of marriage and the Rights Conundrum', in: Mamdani, M. (ed), *Beyond Rights Talk and Culture Talk*, Cape Town: David Philip Publishers, 2000, pp 136–148.

Nussbaum, Martha, *Women and Human Development. The Capabilities Approach*, Cambridge:Cambridge University Press, 2000.

Nyamu, Celestine, 'How should human rights and development respond to cultural legitimization of gender hierarchy in developing countries?', in: *Harvard Int'l L.J.* (2000) 41, pp 381–418.

Okin, Susan Moller, *Justice, gender and the family*, USA: Basic Books Inc., 1989.

Okin, Susan Moller, 'Is multiculturalism bad for women?', in: *Boston Review*, (1997) 22, pp 25–32.

Otto, Dianne, 'Rethinking the "Universality" of Human Rights Law', in: *Columbia Human Rights Law Review*, (1997), 29–1, pp 1–46.

Packer, Corinne A.A., *Using Human Rights to Change Tradition. Traditional practices harmful to women's reproductive health in sub-Saharan Africa*, Antwerp: Intersentia, 2002.

Pateman, Carole, *The Sexual Contract*, Cambridge: Polity Press, 1988.

Peters, A.A.G., 'De emancipatie van de mens', in: Biesheuvel, M.B.W. & Flinterman, C. (eds), *De rechten van de mens*, Amsterdam: Meulenhoff Informatief, 1983, pp 7–22.

Phillips, Anne, 'Religion: ally, threat or just religion', in: Casanova, José & Phillips, Anne, *A Debate on the Public Role of Religion and its Social and Gender Implications.* Programme on Gender and Development, Paper No. 5. Geneva: UNRISD, 2009, pp 39–56.

Phillips, Anne, *Multiculturalism without culture*, Princeton: Princeton University Press, 2007.

Pollis, Adamantia & Schwab, Peter, 'Human Rights: A Western Construct with Limited Applicability', in: Pollis & Schwab (eds), *Human Rights: Cultural and Ideological Perspectives*, New York: Praeger, 1979, pp 1–18.

Raday, Frances, 'Culture, religion and gender', in: 1 *I.CON*, (2003) 4, pp 663–715.

Raday, Frances, 'Culture, Religion, and Cedaw's Article 5(A)', in: Schöpp-Schilling, H. Beate & Flinterman, C. (eds.), *The Circle of Empowerment*, New York: The Feminist Press, 2007, pp 68–85.

Raday, Frances, 'Traditionalist religious and cultural challengers – international and constitutional human rights responses', in: *Isr. L. Rev.* (2008) Vol.41, pp 596–634.

Rehof, Lars Adam, *Guide to the Travaux préparatoires of the United nations Convention on the Elimination of All Forms of Discrimination against Women,* Dordrecht: Martin Nijhoff Publishers, 1993.

Saharso, Sawitri, 'Over de grens: zwarte, migranten en vluchtelingenvrouwen in het debat over multiculturaliteit'. In: Holtmaat, Rikki (ed.) *Een verdrag voor alle vrouwen. Verkenning van de betekenis van het VN-Vrouwenverdrag voor de multiculturele samenleving.* Den Haag: E-Quality, 2002, pp 29–40.

Sano, Hans-Otto, 'Development and Human Rights: The Necessary but Partial Integration of Human Rights and Development', in: *Human Rights Quarterly*, (2000) 22, 734–752.

Schippers, Minneke, *Never Marry a Woman with Big Feet. Women in Proverbs from Around the World*, London and New Haven: Yale University Press, 2005.

Schöpp-Schilling, H. Beate & Flinterman, C. (eds.), *The Circle of Empowerment*, New York: The Feminist Press, 2007.

Sepúlveda, M. Magdalena, *The nature of the obligations under the International Covenant on Economic, Social and Cultural Rights*, Antwerp: Intersentia, 2003.

Shachar, Ayelet, *Multicultural Jurisdictions: Cultural differences and Women's Rights.* Cambridge: Cambridge University Press, 2001.

Smart, Carol, *Feminism and the Power of Law.* London: Routledge, 1989.

Smart, Carol, 'The women in legal discourse', in: *Social and Legal Studies*, (1992) 1, pp 29–44.

Solanka, Iyiola, 'Stigma: A limiting principle allowing multi-consciousness in anti-discrimination law?', in: Schiek, D. & Chege, V. (eds): *European Union Non-Discrimination Law Comparative Perspectives on Multidimensional Equality Law,* London: Routledge 2008, pp 115–136.

Sunder, Madhavi, 'Piercing the veil', in: *Yale Law Journal*, (2003) 112, pp 1399–1472.

Uvin, Peter, 'On High Moral Ground. Incorporation of Human Rights by the Development Enterprise', in: *Praxis*, (2000) Vol. XVII.

Volpp, Leti, 'Blaming Culture for Bad Behaviour', in: *Yale Journal of the Humanities*, (2000) 12, pp 89–115.

Volpp, Leti, 'Feminism versus Multiculturalism', in: *Colombia Law Review*, (2001) 101, pp 1181–1218.

Vreeken, Rob, *Baas in eigen boerka. Van Koran tot girlpower*, Amsterdam: Uitgeverij J.M. Meulenhoff, 2010.

Wallach Scott, Joan, 'Gender: a Useful Category of Historical Analysis' in: *The American Historical Review*, (1986) 91, pp 1053–1075.

Weller, Paul, "'Human Rights', 'Religion' and the 'Secular'", in: Ghanea, Nazila, Stephens, Alan & Walden, Rachel (eds), *Does God believe in Human Rights?* Leiden: Martinus Nijhoff Publishers, 2007, pp 147–179.

Winston, Morton, 'Human Rights as Moral Rebellion and Social Construction', in: *Journal of Human Rights*, (2007) 6, 279–305.

Winter, B., et al, 'The UN approach to harmful traditional practices', in: *International Feminist Journal of Politics*, (2002) 4–1, pp 72–94.

Wohlbold, E., *CEDAW: Shifting the Gaze: Is Article 5(A) an Effective Way of Tackling Issues of Gender Prejudice and Stereotyping?* Masters Thesis, written for the London School of Economics & Political Science (MSc in Gender, Development and Globalization), London: September 2008 (Unpublished, on file with authors.).

Young, Iris Marion, *Justice and the Politics of Difference*, Princeton: Princeton University Press, 1990.